DATE DUE

THE ACTOR'S ART

THE ACTOR'S ART

THEATRICAL REMINISCENCES
METHODS OF STUDY AND
ADVICE TO ASPIRANTS

SPECIALLY CONTRIBUTED BY

LEADING ACTORS OF THE DAY

EDITED BY

J. A. HAMMERTON

PREFATORY NOTE BY SIR HENRY IRVING

BENJAMIN BLOM New York/London

First Published 1897
Reissued 1969 by
Benjamin Blom, Inc., Bronx, New York 10452
and 56 Doughty Street, London, W.C. 1

Library of Congress Catalog Card Number 72-82830

Printed in the United States of America

CONTENTS

PART IV

TWO "SCHOOLS" FOR ACTING

PREFATORY NOTE

This little book seems to me to be an excellent manual of the actor's art. Mr. Hammerton has kept a judicious eye upon essentials; and the experiences he has gathered from exponents of the art of acting ought to be of much practical value to the novice.

Henry Irving.

5 March 1897.

THE ACTOR'S ART

INTRODUCTION

When discussing the purpose of this book with a well-known and veteran actor, the writer was told that "advice" was the last thing budding tragedians were ready to accept; and the veteran proceeded to emphasise his point.

"Young men, nowadays," he said, "think they know a deal more about acting than Irving or Toole, while the average 'old stager' they regard with ill-concealed disdain.

"But," he proceeded, in a reminiscent mood, "I needn't say 'nowadays'; for, to tell the truth, I had a good supply of 'cheek' in my own young days. Why, I wasn't nineteen years of age when I offered to play, for a manager's 'benefit,' a scene from 'Othello' and one from 'Raising the Wind,' in both of which I was to impersonate the leading character! The offer was refused, and I have often thought of the youthful presumption which prompted it."

It was a relief to discover that my veteran did not think "cheek" was exclusively a product of these degenerate days. But in the matter of advice he was profoundly convinced of the truth of the opinion with which our conversation had opened.

"No," he said, "I would not advise any beginner

what to do: it would be useless—absolutely useless;" and he brought his fist down in a manner that plainly said, "This is my opinion, and, *therefore*, the only true opinion!"

Now, my veteran was entirely wrong in supposing that I meant to make this a book of advice; nothing was further from my thoughts, as I afterwards succeeded in convincing him. Experience, and opinions based upon experience, were the objects of my quest; but at the same time I took occasion to disagree with him as to the willingness of young actors to be advised.

Many well-known actor-managers of wide experience have assured me that nothing is more promising for the future of the art than the fact that stage aspirants to-day are really distinguished for the readiness with which they accept the advice of those who have "gone through the mill," and the judicious manner in which they court counsel.

The acceptance of advice largely depends upon the manner in which it is given. If the master impresses his pupil with a sense of his knowledge, but does not make the pupil think that he is being used as a mere foil for his master's vast learning, then will the pupil feel a debt of gratitude to his tutor.

Once again, the object of compiling this book was not to perform the thankless task of gathering advice from the great. It was to bring together some interesting and mainly original, records of dramatic experience, the opinions arising therefrom, and some account of the methods of eminent actors, that the work was undertaken; with a view to presenting the beginner on the stage, the stage aspirant, the amateur actor, and the playgoer, with a book which might be at once helpful and interesting. How far that object has been attained, it is not for me to say.

The form of the work was only decided upon after much cogitation. It may not be the best; but it has proved the most practicable. The book might, with less labour to the compiler, have been made simply an extension of Part III., which comprises a number of special contributions from leading actors of the day; but there is no finality, and much repetition, in the mere multiplication of individual opinion. The brief biographical notices which accompany the various contributions to this section make no pretence to completeness. Indeed, a complete biographical record of a contemporary actor is impossible—it is "out of date" six months or a year after publication. All that has been here attempted, is to touch briefly upon the 'prentice years of the various actors who contribute to the book.

Part I. has been compiled more with a view to focussing professional opinion on the actor's art than for the purpose of expounding the writer's own ideas.

In the second part of the book the lives of three great actors of the past have been treated in a way that, it is hoped, will especially appeal to the stage student: their lives as these affected their art, their ascertained methods of study and preparation, their opinions of the art they practised, have been thrown into relief for the notice of the stage aspirant, while the general reader may not be entirely uninterested.

The concluding part of the book suggested itself to the writer as a suitable "tailpiece"; for it is to such companies as those of Mr. Compton and Mr. Osmond Tearle that the drama looks for its most serviceable recruits, and their views on the actor's apprenticeship are, therefore, well worthy of consideration.

Unlike most books that have been written primarily for the stage student, there is here no vain attempt to teach the art of acting in so many lessons, no endeavour to reduce the complex passions and emotions of the human heart to a "system"; but the writer believes that these pages may afford much useful information to the student, and the young actor may find in them some hints to assist him in the study of his art; though the reading of this, and of every other book on acting, will not make an actor out of one who has no dramatic ability.

J. A. H.

PART I

THE ACTOR'S ART

I

THE ACTOR'S ART

THE art of acting is so wide a subject that several volumes might be devoted to its discussion without prolixity; for the histrionic art not only implies the study of life and character, but the actual interpretation of these. Thus, in giving the present chapter a general heading, it is not to be supposed that a futile attempt is to be made to summarise within its compass the art which has already produced a vast library of books; the intention being merely to formulate some general remarks on a variety of points which are not dealt with in the succeeding chapters.

One of the first things to strike the student of acting is the wonderful universality of the dramatic instinct. It is born in us all, this habit of mimicking others; but latter-day education, which seems admirably designed to stamp out individuality and to reduce all nascent human minds to one dead level of mental mediocrity, soon destroys the mimetic talent by making the child too self-conscious. Of all places in the world, I came across a happy reference to this very point in a religious journal recently. The writer told how, sitting near an open window, he had heard a small boy discourse, in a high-pitched narrative key, to some playmates, as follows:—

"'I was sittin' in my mother's chair,' he stated, 'an'

my sister come into the room, an' said in a narsty, snarly way, "Get out of that chair."

"'My father was in the room, an' he said to me, "Stay where you are till you're asked in a proper manner." So I stayed where I was, an' my sister stood and sulked with a finger in her mouth, scratchin' my sleeve with her other hand. Me an' father didn't take no notice of her, an' all at once she up with my new inkstand off the table an' threw it downstairs. Broken. Then she up with the oranges an' threw them downstairs. One 'it the 'all lamp. Broken.

"'My father stood lookin' on, with his hands in his pockets, an' then he said, "Now, my girl, per'aps you'll go to bed?"

"'Tantrums. Oh, I call 'em tantrums. But there! that's like a girl—if you won't let her do one little thing she wants to do, she does a lot of others *worse*."

"It was inimitably told," says the writer. "He had stopped beneath the window and so graphically had he described the little scene, that it lived. The 'narsty, snarly' way in which the girl spoke; the quiet self-control of the man; the sulky attitude of the girl, with one finger in her mouth, and the vicious hand wanting, yet not daring, to hurt; the ungovernable rage at her own impotence, the recklessness of revenge—all were communicated in the boy's sketch. The comical finality of tone in which he uttered the word 'broken' was as convincing as though he had told you that new inkstands were events in his life. All his dreams of grandeur had gone to pieces with it. *Broken*. You knew how hopeless it was to think of the 'might have been.' And the ''all lamp'—it had cost money, and money was scarce in his home, as he told by the enormity—*Broken*. Where was the use dilating?

"Before a child has become self-conscious, either

through education or other restraint, he is not only forcible, but frequently dramatic and poetical in expression. Fear, affection, grief, anger, and every passing emotion, are presented and emphasised with the instinct to impart and impress the truth. His imagination is vivid, and the creatures of his imagination are as real to him as the creatures of flesh and blood; thus he presents them as absolute facts. His methods differ according to his surroundings; but before self-repression has been taught and acquired, and he reaches a scientific and philosophical standpoint, he will demonstrate his own meaning with an elaboration of detail, with expression, tone, and gesture, which go far to give breadth and finish to the minor part he acts upon life's stage."

Few will hesitate to endorse these remarks; a better little treatise on the dramatic instinct could not have been put in fewer words. The late Cardinal Manning had also noted this universal endowment of childhood; for Miss Mary Anderson (Mrs. Navarro) tells us that he once remarked to her: "From our cradles, we all have a tendency to act. Small boys pretend to be men, soldiers, anything but what they really are. Tiny girls play at being mothers, cradling their dolls. The so-called art of acting increases this tendency in those who witness it almost as much as in those who practise it. I cannot conceive how the latter can escape being led in time to an unconscious development of artificiality or exaggeration in their thoughts, and as a natural result in their speech and manner." While the Cardinal's powers of observation did not err, his conclusion was entirely wrong, for a reason which will presently appear.

Max Nordau, in his book on "Paradoxes," evidently bent on excelling Diderot, touches the art of acting in a very interesting, but most unconvincing manner. He denies "genius" to even the greatest of actors, and genius, in his estimation, is an extraordinary development of the judgment and the will; but in the great actor Nordau recognises "talent," and by talent he means "an equivalent expression for dexterity acquired through a sufficient amount of practice." The actor's "peculiar capacity," he declares, "is due to the development, attained by the exercise of special care, of such organic qualities as appertain to the great majority not only of men but also of the higher animals, namely, the faculty of imitation and the reciprocal action of the conceptions upon the movements and of the movements upon the conceptions." Nordau means by this that the outward expression of an emotion will lead to its inward realisation; that is to say, that to imitate the physical movements of laughter will produce a feeling of elation in the mind; while to simulate the frown and attitude of anger will make the actor really feel angry. "Every one," continues Nordau, "has it in his power to make the following experiment—first of all, to determine by what movements in his case the mental affection of profound grief attains to visible expression, whether, for instance, by bowing down of the head, by some particular expression, some particular tone of the voice, sobs, &c.; and then to imitate accurately all these muscular movements. If he does this he will very soon notice, probably to his astonishment, that he has become of a profoundly sorrowful temperament. . . . It must always be kept in mind that the nerves which lead from the outer limits of the body to the centres, as well as those very centres and the nerves which run from them to other centres or to muscles, all form one single apparatus, the connections of which have become organic and automatic, and that the apparatus goes through the whole cycle of its automatic work, no matter at what point it may happen to be set in motion, and that, too, either in the proper sequence or in a reverse direction, by way of conception to movement, or by way of movement to conception." Having stated his paradox, Nordau is not the man to shrink from its application, and so he naturally sets down his opinion that "most distinguished adopters of men's parts are just those who must be of a subordinate class of mind, have an empty consciousness and a stunted personality;" while "the distinguished actor has most emphatically the psychological disposition of the child and of the savage."

Now, Nordau and Cardinal Manning both make similar mistakes. Without Nordau's elaborate process of reasoning the Cardinal jumped to the conclusion that, because it was an actor's business to impersonate other characters, he became a confirmed actor, so to speak, and was never himself, even off the boards; on the same principle that the dyer's hand is subdued to the element in which it works. Nordau thinks that the best actor is the most thoughtless, the most characterless man, as the greatest obstacle to the actor's faithful reproduction of passions or emotions, in accordance with the theory of the German savant, is "cogitational activity." He seems to believe, in fact, that an actor is a man with an undeveloped brain. On his theory we should have to say of a splendid old actor, that he had "a young head on old shoulders!" Cardinal Manning forgot, or failed to understand, that the first essential to "the so-called art of acting" is *subordination* of self—not *annihilation* of self. We have all seen a score or two of Hamlets, and in every case the actor has subordinated himself more or less to the character assumed; yet there has been something different in every one of these Hamlets; something indefinable, but something real. This is the actor's indestructible, insuppressible individuality, making itself felt by means which lie outside of art and come direct from nature. As a matter of fact, the great actor is generally a great individuality, and a great individuality could not hide itself off the stage, even "unconsciously," as Manning suggested, in "artificiality"; indeed, it is a fine point whether it is within the bounds of possibility for any one to be *unconsciously artificial*—artificiality being the result of extreme self-consciousness. Although the actor impersonates many characters, he never loses his own; but merely sinks it while on the stage.

Nordau, through obvious ignorance of the art of acting, makes the mistake of assuming that, because an actor may be a perfect Proteus, he has no individuality of his own. The German philosopher has observed the mimetic powers of children, like the writer previously quoted; but, unlike him, he has rashly concluded that the actor is an adult with the "psychological disposition of the child." He neglects to inquire into the *motive* of the child-*mimic* as compared with that of the adult *actor*. The importance of this point must be apparent. The child is totally unconscious of all its gestures and attitudes so long as it does not feel that it is being critically observed; and immediately it *feels* that its actions are being scrutinised, grace gives way to gaucherie. But the actor has to be consciously unconscious (I suppose I may be permitted a paradox as well as Diderot or Nordau); he has to *consciously* imitate the gestures and attitudes which in the child are the result of no artistic effort; he has to be as "natural" as the child by means of consummate art; he has to *appear* to believe in fictions of the brain in which the child actually does *believe*. These things make a wonderful difference, and these things are all ignored by Nordau. On his theory, Master Betty, the famous boy-actor, should have developed into a great adult actor, whereas he was not even mediocre when he grew to man's estate. Possibly, Nordau might claim Master Betty as proof, and suggest that his failure as an adult was because he had outgrown the actor's mind which he possessed when a boy! The fact is, that Betty, like all infant phenomena, performed, when a boy, with no intelligent purpose, merely exercising an unusual gift of mimicry in accordance with certain directions from one in whose counsel he had absolute *faith*. When a man, and called upon to act in accordance with the conceptions of his mind founded upon his author's text, he proved lacking in those imaginative qualities which the true artist must possess, and was, consequently, unable to *convince* a public which, on account of his extreme youth, he had previously *interested*. Master Betty, it may be mentioned, played Hamlet after three nights' "study": Betterton said that after fifty years of Hamlet he had not even then fathomed the profoundest depths of its philosophy!

The "natural" actor is really the greatest artist, and the child-actor can, by no process of reason, be regarded as an artist in any sense of the word. Talma says: "I have suffered cruel losses, and have often been assailed with profound sorrows; but after the first moment, when grief vents itself in cries and tears, I have found myself involuntarily turning my gaze inwards ('*je faisais un retour sur mes souffrances*'), and found the actor was unconsciously studying the man, and catching nature in the act." Here we see the artistic temperament in action. Is the "psychological disposition" of a Talma the same as that of a Master Betty? Nordau asks us to believe it is, and Manning inferred the same thing. The idea is too absurd to be entertained for a moment. "The actor's art," says Macready, "is to fathom the depth of character, to trace its latent motive, to feel its finest quiverings of emotion, to comprehend the thoughts that are hidden under words, and thus possess one's soul of the actual mind of the individual man." It is the height of folly to suppose that the child-actor can have the remotest conception of such an art; and as a matter of fact, the infant histrionic phenomenon is nothing more or less than an exceptionally clever mimic, or a very graceful little automaton; an "actor," in the true sense of the word, he cannot possibly be; for the actor must have intelligence and understanding, and these are impossible to the mind of a child of five, or even ten, years of age.

One of those "popular" papers, that pretend to know everything about everything and everybody, published some time ago the following alleged statement from "a popular actress" to one of its contributors:—

"Owing to the possession of a very bad memory, the learning of a new part is a tedious operation to me, and it sometimes takes me weeks to master the words only. I have frequently heard it asserted that, by constant practice, the memory may be greatly improved, but this has not happened in my case. I have tried one or two 'systems,' but I think they made matters worse instead of better.

"As a rule, I carry a copy of my part about with me, and study it whenever I get a moment's leisure. My method is very simple, and consists in repeating a great many times each sentence. My bad memory has been the means of my losing many opportunities, as it precludes me entirely from 'winging,' that is to say, taking up a part at, perhaps, an hour's notice, and learning one's portion [1] of it bit by bit, as required. It is extremely difficult to do this, and there are few actresses in London who are proficient in the art."

One need have little hesitation in branding this as an invention, or referring to the "popular" actress as a silly

[1] What, by the way, is one's "portion" of a "part"?

chatterbox. If there is a "popular" actress in London capable of talking such drivel, then is the art in a parlous condition. Why, the method of learning a part as here described is the method by which a parrot learns to speak. This alleged "popular" actress is made to say that the be-all and end-all of acting is the correct repetition of words; and that the one great, nay, the only, essential is a good memory. I fear that if this actress does exist, and if she is really "popular," and if she did actually say the words attributed to her, we must look for her on the burlesque stage, where opulence of animal qualities is worth more than the brain of a Rachel or an Ellen Terry. Words, as Tennyson has beautifully said, "half reveal and half conceal the soul within." It is the actor's office to so utilise all the resources of his art that "the soul within" may be wholly revealed; and to this end the mere mechanical repetition of words is of absolutely no avail.

Others again fall into the error of thinking that great actors trust to the "inspiration of the moment." As Sir Henry Irving says: "Nothing can be more erroneous. There will, of course, be such moments, when an actor at a white heat illuminates some passages with a flash of imagination (and this mental condition, by the way, is impossible to the student sitting in his arm-chair); but the great actor's surprises are generally well weighed, studied, and balanced. We know that Edmund Kean constantly practised before a mirror effects which startled his audience by their apparent spontaneity. It is the accumulation of such effects which enables an actor, after many years, to present many great characters with remarkable completeness." The consummate artist will produce what are seemingly accidental effects by long and careful study, and thus make "art conceal art"; but he will never trust to the inspiration of the moment, which Lewes aptly likens to "trusting to a shipwreck for your first lesson in swimming."

Even the greatest actors have their limitations; though these are mainly physical. Lewes emphasises the necessity of actors "restricting themselves to parts for which they have the *physical* qualifications. Acting being personation," says Lewes, "it is clear that, unless the actor has the personal qualifications requisite for the representation of the character, no amount of ability in conceiving the part will avail." But the great actors are precisely those who realise their own limitations, and never attempt a part in which they do not feel confident of success. Many great actors have triumphed, of course, over physical shortcomings by sheer weight of genius. Betterton was by no means an Adonis; Garrick was short and slight; Macklin was positively ugly; Kean was insignificant of figure, "with a voice harsh and discordant in its upper register"; Talma's face was round and flat, his figure short and thick, and his voice "only remarkable for its strength and depth"; and so on *ad infinitum.* But all these actors had genius, and where that is absent the physique of the actor becomes a more vital consideration.

Attempts to found public academies for instruction in the histrionic art have been made scores of times since Shakespeare's day, but never with any degree of success. Garrick, during his management of Drury Lane, once had a small dramatic class of children, whom he brought out in a little piece which he had written for them; but Miss Pope was the only valuable actress who came out of this school, and Garrick seems to have made it a hobby rather than a serious attempt to found a dramatic school. Macklin suggested to Garrick the opening of a sort of academy, but was not encouraged in the idea by the amiable David. He tried the experiment himself, however, and brought out Foote and Dr. Hill. But Macklin was always instructing aspirants for the stage, and a very curious picture of his method is given in John O'Keefe's "Recollections." Macklin's pupils, Miss Ambrose and Mr. Glenville, came for instruction to his house in Dorset Street, Dublin, "far on as you go to Drumcondra," his residence being next to a nunnery. "In Macklin's garden there were three long parallel walks, and his method of exercising their voices was thus: his two young pupils with backboards (such as they use in boarding-schools) walked firmly, slow, and well, up and down the two side walks; Macklin himself paraded the centre walk. At the end of every twelve paces he made them stop, and, turning gracefully, the young actor called out across the walk, 'How do you do, Miss Ambrose?' She answered, 'Very well, I thank you, Mr. Glenville!' They then took a few more paces, and the next question was, 'Do you not think it a very fine day, Mr. Glenville?' 'A very fine day indeed, Miss Ambrose!' was the answer. Their walk continued; and then, 'How do you do, Mr. Glenville?' 'Pretty well, I thank you, Miss Ambrose!' And this exercise continued for an hour or so (Macklin still keeping in the centre walk), in the full hearing of their religious next-door neighbours. Such was Macklin's method of training the management of the voice; if too high, too low, a wrong accent, or a faulty inflection, he immediately noticed it, and made them repeat the words twenty times till all was right." This scarcely strikes one as an ideal method of bringing out the dramatic abilities of a stage aspirant;[1] but Macklin had consider-

[1] Macklin, it is chronicled, would say to a candidate, putting forward his repellent face, "Look at me!" "First, sir," he would croak, "you should have a *silvery voice;* and secondly, sir, *a pleasing face!*"

able success as a theatrical tutor, or "stage coach," though he never was able to completely realise his dream of a Thespian Academy. Who that ever dreamt of such a thing has been able to realise it?

One of the most ambitious attempts was made by Dr. Aaron Hill, already mentioned as a pupil of Macklin. His project was nothing less than a "tragic academy." He was going to do wonders with it, revivify the drama, elevate and improve the art of acting, and produce his own tragedy, "Zara," an indifferent adaptation of Voltaire's "Zaïre." This was in 1733, and two years later he was still fishing for "patrons." He had come to the conclusion, however, that unless he took the main burden of the risk of the enterprise himself it would never become an accomplished fact, and all that he now desired was that a certain number of great men might patronise him so far as adhibiting their names to the following declaration: "Whereas certain gentlemen have promised at their own expense to attempt an improvement, under the name of a Tragic Academy, for extending and regulating theatrical diversions, and for instructing and educating actors in the practice of dramatic passions, and a power to express them strongly, the success of which laudable purpose might establish the reputation of the stage by appropriating its influence to the service of wisdom and virtue; our names are therefore subscribed in declaration that we will protect and give countenance to this useful undertaking so long as the same shall be carried on with a skill and attention correspondent to the proposal." But the worldly great refused Dr. Hill even this poor service; Frederick, Prince of Wales, whose patronage it was hoped would launch the scheme into the waters of success, latterly declined to identify himself with the project, and eventually we find the doctor throwing up the academic sponge, renouncing his interest in the stage, and leaving the theatres to their "modish frequenters," and the "fools of fashion." But, during the century and a half which have passed since then, it cannot be said that the dramatic art has been seriously affected by the failure of this scheme for a "tragic academy."

Sheridan also projected an "oratorical academy," and was heartily encouraged in his project by Lord Chesterfield, who agreed to be a patron, and subscribed—a guinea! Even this lordly support did not avail, and the scheme withered in the bud. Macready had a project for a "commonwealth of players," which also came to naught; but it would be tiresome to merely enumerate the scores of projected Thespian academies that have never had a "local habitation and a name," and those that have been started only to die in infancy, over whose graves it might be written—

> "Since it is so soon I'm done for,
> What on earth was I begun for?"

Suffice it to say, that of recent years there has been less talk about dramatic academies, possible or impossible; a fact which manifests a better appreciation of the art; for it may be confidently said that the theatric art is too wide, too diversified, too universal, to lend itself to the trammels of an academy. The study of human life is too vast a subject to be reduced to academic confines, and hence the invariable and certain failure of all schemes to rear an academy to Thespis, other than the incomparable university of human experience.

Academies of any kind are the least praiseworthy feature of civilisation; their *raison d'être* is to dignify mediocrity and incapacity with a spurious reputation. Haydon declared that "academies all over Europe were signals of distress thrown out to stop the decay of art."

While it may be argued that this says nothing to the discredit of academies, it implies that academies mark the decay, rather than the advance, of art, and if that be so, academies can do little or nothing to prevent the decay which brings them into existence. It is always at a time when there is a "slump" in the legitimate drama that the idea of a Thespian academy comes to the front, and this fact alone is suggestive. Dr. Waagen held that "the academic system gave artificial elevation to mediocrity; that it deadened natural talent, and introduced into the freedom of art an unsalutary degree of authority and interference." Now, there is no art in which freedom is so necessary as in the theatric art; and, on Dr. Waagen's proposition, academic interference with the art of acting would only hasten its decay. Even Macready, who, as has been mentioned, half entertained a notion of a kind of school, or commonwealth, of players, condemned the Paris Conservatoire. Writing of a visit paid to it in 1845, he says: "Heard the pupils of Samson go through their course of theatrical instruction. It is an institution of the Government to train pupils, who are elected to the school, for the stage. I was interested, and saw the inefficiency of the system clearly; it was teaching *conventionalism*—it was perpetuating the mannerism of the French stage, which is all mannerism. Genius would be cramped, if not maimed and distorted, by such a course."

This is the inevitable conclusion; the art of acting is not for academies; the actor's university is the world; all that can be taught is well taught already—fencing, calisthenics, dancing, elocution, language, &c.—but these are the merest bare bones of art. Acting is not decaying; it can only decay with the decay of national character; when decay sets in there, all the academies in the country will not be able to avert the *débâcle*.

II

"LEARN TO FEEL"

In addressing his poem, "The Actor," to his friend, Bonnel Thornton, Robert Lloyd touches on the difficulty of teaching the art of acting, and while admitting that certain general principles may be laid down, he considers that the best method of applying these must be discovered by the theatrical aspirant himself. He says—

> "Acting, dear Thornton, its perfection draws
> From no observance of mechanic laws:
> No settled maxims of a favourite stage,
> No rules delivered down from age to age,
> Let players nicely mark them as they will,
> Can e'er entail hereditary skill.
>
> . . . . .
>
> Perfection's top with weary toil and pain,
> 'Tis genius only that can hope to gain.
> The play'r's profession (though I hate the phrase,
> 'Tis so mechanic in these modern days)
> Lies not in trick, or attitude, or start;
> Nature's true knowledge is the only art.
> The strong-felt passion bolts into his face;
> The mind untouched, what is it but grimace?
> To this one standard make your just appeal,
> Here lies the golden secret: Learn to feel.
> Or fool, or monarch, happy or distrest,
> No actor pleases that is not *possessed*."

There is no doubt that Lloyd states a great truth when he says—

> "Here lies the golden secret: LEARN TO FEEL."

But feeling is not everything, as Lloyd acknowledges further on—

> "The player's province they but vainly try
> Who want these powers—Deportment, Voice, and Eye."

Students of the stage are well aware that there has long existed considerable difference of opinion on this very question; and Diderot, who asserted that the greatest actor is he who is himself unmoved in the very height of the passion he is mimicking upon the stage, has many believers even to-day. It may not be unprofitable, therefore, to devote some attention to this point.

"Extreme sensibility," says Diderot, in his *Paradoxe sur le Comédien*, "makes middling actors; middling sensibility makes the ruck of bad actors; a complete absence of sensibility paves the way for the sublime actor." The key to this enigma lies, of course, in the definition of "sensibility" as understood by Diderot, and here is the key: "Sensibility," says Diderot, "is that disposition which accompanies organic weakness, mobility of the diaphragm, vivacity of the imagination, delicacy of the nerves, which inclines one to . . . loss of self-control, to exaggeration, to contempt, to disdain, to obtuseness to the true, the good, and the beautiful, to injustice, to madness." As Mr. William Archer says, the conditions here described might be more correctly defined as hysteria; and if Diderot argued that "the great actor must not be hysterical," then all would be agreed. But while Diderot destroys his paradox in rashly venturing upon a definition of sensibility, it is plain that he considers a great actor should not "feel" his part, and that the actor who enters into the spirit of the character he assumes is no true artist. This affords us a clearly-defined starting point. *Is* the golden secret: "LEARN TO FEEL"? What is the verdict of the actors?

In his scholarly little work on the psychology of acting, "Masks or Faces?" Mr. Archer has collected a formidable volume of evidence, from which I shall presently quote, against the theory expounded by Diderot, and largely accepted among French actors. But it has always been notorious that the best of actors have been accustomed to participate in the feelings of the characters they have been for the time assuming. Betterton, we are told, was not merely the character he pretended to be on the stage, but all the evening; so was Mrs. Siddons; and so, too, it is said, was Lekain, though in his case it is doubtful. Garrick, however, could forget Lear to set a group in the green-room laughing at a good story; but he was often affected by the emotion of his part to the point of weeping. Mrs. Siddons, likewise, entered personally into the passions of her part, although she belonged more to the "classical" than to the "life" school of acting. Dr. Doran says that, "In the pretended fainting scene of Arpasia in "Tamerlane," after the wild cry, 'Love! Death! Moneses!' Mrs. Siddons fell back, violently clutching her drapery, and her dress all disordered—a swoon in earnest, which caused a rush from the pit and boxes of part of the excited and sympathising audience. The agitation of the actress was almost perilous to her life!" Madame Sarah Bernhardt also confesses that when her "personage" weeps, she weeps too; and there are innumerable instances, both of present-day actors and those of the past, who have declared themselves to be personally affected in moving situations which have been summoned up by the instrumentality of their art. We will cite several distinguished witnesses.

Campbell, in his "Life" of Mrs. Siddons, quotes that great actress's very curious study of the character of Constance in "King John." "If the representative of Constance," writes Mrs. Siddons, "shall ever forget, even behind the scenes, those disastrous events which impel her to break forth into the overwhelming effusions of wounded friendship, disappointed ambition, and maternal tenderness, upon the first moment of her appearance in the third act, when stunned with terrible surprise, she exclaims—

> 'Gone to be married—gone to swear a peace!
> False blood to false blood joined—gone to be friends.'

If, I say, the mind of the actress for one moment wanders from these distressing events, she must inevitably fall short of that high and glorious colouring which is indispensable to the painting of this magnificent portrait. . . . Whenever I was called upon to impersonate the character of Constance, I never, from the beginning of the play to the end of my part in it, once suffered my dressing-room door to be closed, in order that my attention might constantly be fixed on these distressing events, which, by this means, I could plainly hear going on upon the stage, the terrible effects of which progress were to be represented by me. Moreover, I never omitted to place myself, with 'Arthur' in my hand, to hear the word, when, upon the reconciliation of England and France, they enter the gates of Angiers to ratify the contract of marriage between the Dauphin and Lady Blanche; because the sickening sounds of that march would usually cause the bitter tears of rage, disappointment, betrayed confidence, baffled ambition, and, above all, the agonising feelings of maternal affection, to gush into my eyes. In short, the spirit of the whole drama took possession of my mind and frame, by my attention being incessantly riveted to the passing scenes. . . . I have no doubt that the observance of such circumstances, however irrelevant they may appear upon a cursory view, were (*sic*) powerfully aidant in the representations of those expressions of passion in the remainder of this scene, which have been only in part considered." This leaves us in no doubt as to whether Mrs. Siddons believed the actress should experience to some extent the emotions of the character she is portraying.

Miss Helen Faucit (Lady Martin) also relates some experiences of her own, which show how thoroughly this gifted lady is a believer in the actress entering into the spirit and emotions of her part. A few days after learning of the death of a dearly-loved sister, she had to appear at a charity performance in some scenes from "Romeo and Juliet," much against her will, the interests of the charity being the only thing that induced her to make the effort. "I got on very well," she writes, "in the scene with the Friar. There was despair in it, but nothing that in any way touched upon my own trial. My great struggle was in Juliet's chamber when left alone. Then her desolation, her loneliness, became mine, and the rushing tears would have way. Happily the fearful images presented to Juliet's mind of what is before her in the tomb soon sent softer feelings away; but how glad I was when the fancied sight of Tybalt's ghost allowed the grief that was in my heart to find vent in a wild cry of anguish, as well as horror!" Again, writing of her first performance of "The Lady of Lyons," Lady Martin says: "As I recalled to Claude, in bitter scorn, his glowing description of his Palace by the Lake of Como, I broke into a paroxysm of hysterical laughter, which came upon me, I suppose, as the natural relief from the intensity of the mingled feelings of anger, scorn, wounded pride, and outraged love, by which I found myself carried away. The effect upon the audience was electrical, because the impulse was genuine. But well do I remember Mr. Macready's remonstrance with me for yielding to it. It was too daring, he said; to have failed in it might have ruined the scene (which was true). No one, moreover, should ever, he said, hazard an unrehearsed effect. I could only answer that I could not help it; that this seemed the only way for my feelings to find vent; and if the impulse seized me again, again, I feared, I must act the scene in the same way. And often as I have played Pauline, never did the scene fail to bring back the same burst of hysterical emotion; nor, so far as I know, did any of my critics regard my yielding to it as out of place, or otherwise than true to nature."

"The performance of a moving situation," says Mrs. Bancroft, "without the true ring of sensibility in the actor, must fail to affect any one. An emotional break in the voice must be brought about naturally, and by a true appreciation of the sentiment, or what does it become? I can only compare it to a bell with a wooden tongue—it makes a sound, but there it ends. I cannot simulate suffering without an honest sympathy with it. I hold that without great nervous sensibility no one can act pathos. It is impossible to feel the sentiments one has to utter, and but half the author's meaning can be conveyed. It is a casket with the jewel absent. The voice in emotion must be prompted by the heart, and if that is 'out of tune and harsh,' why, then, indeed, the voice is 'like sweet bells jangled.' Art *should* help nature, but nature *must* help art. They are twin sisters, and should go hand in hand, but nature must be the first-born. I was once much impressed by a small child's criticism. He watched for a long time silently and attentively a scene of great emotional interest between two people. When asked what he thought of it, he answered, 'I like that one best.' 'Why?' 'She speaks like telling the truth, and the other speaks like telling lies.' What criticism can be finer than this? One was acting straight from the heart, the other from not even next door but one to it."

"Yes," writes Mr. Wilson Barrett to Mr. Archer, "tears come to my eyes unbidden when I am acting at my best. With an effort I can repress them, but if I am not sufficiently in my part for them to come uncalled, no power of mine can bring them. If one night I have to simulate what I felt the night before, I should certainly expect the effect to be lessened. But mere feeling unguided by art is seldom, if ever, effective. Art without feeling is better than that, but feeling with art is better than both. The most sensitive organisation, coupled with the highest art, makes the greatest actor. In America you will hear the remark, 'Yes, he's a fine artist, but he has no magnetism.' In London you will hear people say, 'Yes, he's a capital actor, but somehow he never touches me.' The meaning is the same; the fine artist is watched and admired, and often he will get the most praise. He has not stirred the emotions of his audience, and they have had ample time to watch his art. But the actor who feels deeply and guides his emotions by his art will draw to see him hundreds to the other's units."

"Whether tears do or do not come readily to the eyes," says Mr. Beerbohm Tree, "will depend upon the mere physical development of the individual. Some people have sensitive lachrymal glands, which may be affected by the simple test of the onion—apply the vegetable and the tears will flow. Others, again, have not this physical sensitiveness. It is, therefore, only possible to speak from personal experience. Tears do undoubtedly arise to my eyes in moving situations, perhaps less readily on the stage than in private contemplation. I do not believe that any emotion can be satisfactorily portrayed outside unless the inside emotion exists also; and I think that the effect upon an audience will generally be in proportion to the power of self-excitation possessed by the actor—given, of course, equal advantages in the way of physique, voice, &c."

Mr. Lionel Brough, who, though best known as a comic actor, has, as Mr. Archer says, every claim to be heard on the question of pathos, writes as follows: "In moving situations I always cry. I can't help it. My voice goes of its own accord. In a certain pathetic scene of a melodrama, which I played in Liverpool with Miss Phillis Hill, we used every night to agree 'not to make fools of ourselves,' as we called it; and every night there would be mutual recriminations at the end of the scene, as, 'I thought you promised me you wouldn't cry?' Answer, in the same tearful voice (with all the make-up washed off), 'So did you, stupid.' But neither of us ever regretted the tears, or the way in which the scene went with the audience. If ever I play a pathetic scene with a child (and in most cases with a woman), I am sure to cry. With men, not so; as in any domestic trouble of my own I should endeavour to restrain my tears in telling my sorrows to a man, but should give them free vent in the presence of the other sex. I don't think an actor ever can be said to play pathos properly unless he feels."

Sir Henry Irving has touched upon this question of sensibility several times, and always with complete conviction. Thus he says: "Diderot laid down a theory that an actor never feels the part he is acting. It is, of course, true that the pain he suffers is not real pain, but I leave it to any one who has ever felt his own heart touched by the woes of another to say, if he can even imagine a case where the man who follows in minutest detail the history of an emotion, from its inception onward, is the only one who cannot be stirred by it—more especially when his own individuality must, perforce, be merged in that of the archetypal sufferer."

Before such an array of evidence—which might be augmented indefinitely—the occasional instances where the superconsciousness of the mind appears in marked contrast with the simulated passion count for little or nothing. Diderot makes the mistake of taking such exceptional cases and building his theory on them. When Edmund Kean and his son Charles were playing in "The Fall of Tarquin," at the Glasgow Theatre, on the first of October 1828, the great tragedian is said to have entered into his part with much of his old vigour, and when in the great judgment scene, mastered by the conflicting passions that assailed him, he fell upon his son's neck with "Pity thy wretched father!" the audience could only find vent for the pent-up feelings with which they had witnessed the scene in peals of applause. Delighted with the effect produced, Kean is said to have whispered to his son, "We are doing the trick, Charlie." But what does this prove? Diderot would say his theory. It only shows that while Kean was in full sympathy with the character he represented, he never forgot that he was *only* representing it; he retained possession of his own mind while he entered into the personation of another individual. For the secret lies midway between the emotionalist and the Diderot theory. To surrender one's self *entirely* to the passions of the character assumed would be false to art and disastrous to the actor; while to represent emotions which one did not understand, not having felt, would be false to nature and, therefore, opposed to art.

Talma has shown more intelligence in discussing this subject than any other French actor. He says: "Oui, nous devons être sensibles, nous devons éprouver l'émotion; mais pour mieux l'imiter, pour mieux en saisir les caractères par l'étude et la réflexion. Notre art en exige de profonds. Point d'improvisation possible sur la scène sous peine d'échec. Tout est calculé, tout doit être prévu, et l'émotion qui semble soudaine, et le trouble quit paraît involontaire. L'intonation, le geste, le regard qui semblent inspirés, ont été répétés cent fois." Here is the thing in a nutshell—the actor must experience emotion and sympathise with the character he is portraying, but only to enable him the better to perfect his study.

The whole question is admirably summed up by Lewes in the following luminous passage, with which we may take leave of the subject:—

"It is a question of *degree.* As in all art, feeling lies at the root, but the foliage and flowers, though deriving their sap from emotion, derive their form and structure from the intellect. The poet cannot write while his eyes are full of tears, while his nerves are trembling from the mental shock, and his hurrying thoughts are too agitated to settle into definite tracks. But he must have felt, or his verse will be a mere echo. It is from the memory of past feelings that he draws the beautiful image with which he delights us. He is tremulous again under the remembered agitation, but it is a pleasant tremor, and in no way disturbs the clearness of his intellect. He is a spectator of his own tumult; and though moved by it, can yet so master it as to select from it only those elements which suit his purpose. We are all spectators of ourselves; but it is the peculiarity of the artistic nature to indulge in such introspection even in moments of all but the most disturbing passion, and to draw thence materials for art. . . . The answer to the question, How far does the actor feel? is, therefore, something like this: He is in a state of emotional excitement sufficiently strong to furnish him with the elements of expression, but not strong enough to disturb his consciousness of the fact that he is only imagining—sufficiently strong to give the requisite tone to his voice and aspect to his features, but not strong enough to prevent his modulating the one and arranging the other according to a preconceived standard. His passion must be ideal—sympathetic, not personal."

III

THE ART OF SPEAKING

"Words fitly spoken are like apples of gold in pictures of silver."

THE ability to speak correctly—by which is meant, to give every spoken word its relative value in emphasis, to accentuate the proper syllables, and to pronounce each word as orthoepy demands—should be one of the first essentials in any person aspiring to histrionic distinction. But with the English as a race the art of speaking has never been very seriously cultivated, and at the present time, perhaps, less than ever. It seems unpatriotic to make such a statement, but our patriotism must not blind us to our faults as a people, and one of these undoubtedly is a deplorable slovenliness of speech. It is not too much to say that thousands of Englishmen who pride themselves on their proficiency in French, German, or Italian, have not yet mastered their mother-tongue. How seldom do we meet a man whose speech is free from provincialisms or Cockneyisms, whose words are spoken as they ought to be, his pronunciation correct, and his emphasis made to reflect the varying strength of the opinions he endeavours to enunciate? It may not be surprising, therefore, that the art of speech, so grossly abused or neglected by our orators, our barristers, and by the common people, should not receive adequate attention at the hands of our actors—although, be it said, it is only on the stage that there appears to be any attempt towards the cultivation of this most delightful art.

It may be urged by some that if the player's province is "to hold, as 'twere, the mirror up to nature," he only reflects the manners of his time in his slipshod utterance. But this is not a tenable argument; for though the player should hold the mirror up to nature, he should *idealise* all he does, not *familiarise.* This is the stumbling-block with superficial critics: this confusion between the ideal—the "realistic," if you will—and the familiar. Many actors, endeavouring to get nearer to nature, mistake faults for beauties, and end by becoming familiar and inartistic. The logical outcome of familiar acting would be to speak on the stage *exactly* as you speak in the drawing-room or in the smoking-room; that is to say, mumble and stammer, and talk so that only your *tête-à-tête* can hear. That, in the opinion of some, would, no doubt, be pure, unadulterated nature on the stage—it would be as near to art as the "real water," "real horses," and "real engines" of melodrama are. Shakespeare's plays hold the mirror up to nature in a way that is at once the admiration and despair of all modern dramatists; yet he makes his characters, pulsing as they are with human passions, speak in a musical blank verse such as human being never naturally used. This is the poet's art: he holds us enchained with the beauty of his diction and the reality of his creations. So should the actor aim at perfection in his speech; for in the mastery of the art of speaking lies the key which will unlock the inmost treasure-house of the poet's mind. But no one seriously denies the necessity of the actor who wishes to secure the highest effect that his primal art and its auxiliaries can obtain, devoting much of his time and thought to the art of speaking.

Up to the early years of the present century the rule on the English stage was, with notable exceptions, to chant the words of the poet with absolutely no regard to sense or sensibility; to maintain a "dead level of declamation." In an old "Life of Betterton" this stupid practice is referred to in these sensible words: "This stiff uniformity of voice is not only displeasing to the ear, but disappoints the effect of the discourse on the hearers; first, by an equal way of speaking, when the pronunciation has everywhere, in every word and every syllable, the same sound, it must inevitably render all parts of speech equal, and so put them on a very unjust level. So that the power of the reasoning part, the lustre and ornament of the figures, the heart, warmth, and vigour of the passionate part being expressed all in the same tone, are flat and insipid, and lost in a supine, or at least unmusical, pronunciation. So that, in short, that which ought to strike and stir up the affections, because it is spoken all alike, without any distinction or variety, moves them not at all." The condition of speech on the English stage to-day, far though it be from perfection, represents, at least, an approximation thereto compared with that which obtained up to the beginning of the century.

There is an erroneous impression abroad that excellence of speech is a gift, not an acquirement—"the gift o' the gab," as it is called in the North. But such is not the case. By diligence and practice one may so gain command over his voice that he may hold thousands by his oratory where, before, he could not have retained the attention of a small audience. Demosthenes laboured under natural impediment of speech and extreme nervousness, yet, by sheer force of will and determination to excel, coupled with constant and unwearied practice, he became a veritable prince of orators; and many a famous orator since has been made out of the most unpromising material. The reason is, that speech is mechanically produced by the voice, which is really an exquisite instrument that may be made to respond to the feelings of its possessor, and to vibrate under his control. By practice one may learn to play upon the harp, to strike sweet sounds from chords upon which one had previously been able only to produce a rude discord; so is it with the voice. By practice and study one may learn to use it with an effect which at first may seem hopelessly beyond attainment. Hence, it follows, that in devoting time and thought to the perfection of his power of speech the young actor is engaging in something which is bound to prove profitable to him in his profession.

In acquiring the art of speaking, one of the first things to be practised is breathing, which should nearly always be performed through the nostrils. The management of the breath is all-important. Upon this the voice depends, and if the voice cannot be sustained, then all is lost. At the time of Garrick's first appearance in London he had not attained proficiency in this respect, and so, at the most critical part, he was growing hoarser and hoarser, and would have been overpowered, but for the efficacy of a Seville orange given him by Dryden Leach, the printer, who used to boast how he had thus contributed to the success of "the great Garrick." This may seem a small thing, but life and art are made up of small things. We know how the loss of a horse-shoe nail affected the fate of a kingdom, and the fable of the lion and the mouse is directly in point. Signor Crivelli, in his work on the art of singing, submits the following rules for the management of the breath, and although they are intended for singers, they are equally applicable to actors and orators: "The clear and elastic vibration of sounds depends on the art of breathing gently, never forcing the breath in the production of the voice, but always sparing it in such a manner that the fibres and muscles of the throat may not be irritated. Thus, knowing how to spare and make good use of the breath is of the greatest importance, as from this is derived the power of sustaining the sounds—of sending forth the voice in the most energetic or in the most delicate manner—so as to express with true colouring whatever emotion or passion the poet and composer may wish to describe."

For all practical purposes the voice may be regarded as being composed of two classes of organs: the lower, vibrating organs; and the upper, articulating organs. "The lower," says one authority, "are the larynx and glottis, with all their muscles, chords, and ligaments, which produce the voice. The upper are the throat, palate, tongue, teeth, and lips, which combine to articulate the words we utter with the voice." These being all purely physical attributes, it follows that they are capable of development by studious practice, just as the mind is by culture, and the body by exercise.

With those who live by the use of their voice, or those who cultivate its use for the pleasure so afforded, the voice should be as judiciously and as constantly exercised as is the body with the professional or amateur athlete. This is always taken for granted in the case of singers; but it is frequently ignored in the case of actors and orators. And until actors as a class come to realise that the mere use of the voice on the stage each evening is not sufficient to keep so delicate an instrument in proper condition, we shall make little further progress towards perfection in the art of speaking. What would we think of the singer who never did more than hum over his pieces in private and at rehearsal, and trusted to his voice to take every note accurately when on the concert platform? Yet many actors, in the belief that speaking is the common gift of all—greater in some, less in others—are content to rely upon an untrained, undeveloped, and unpractised voice to reflect all the subtle meanings of the author's text. Is it any wonder that they fail so frequently?

Just as the mechanism of the human voice may be divided into two classes, so may its sound be divided into three registers: the middle, the higher, and the lower; or the natural or chest voice, the falsetto or head voice, and the orotund or deeper voice. Of these, Canon Fleming, a reliable authority on this subject, says: "The high voice is that which we use in calling to some one at a distance. The low voice is that which is formed deep in the throat, and which in its final words approaches towards a whisper. The natural voice is that in which mainly we all speak, or ought to speak—the tone in which we generally converse, and in which we should read. This is sometimes called 'level speaking.' We are all endowed (there are some exceptions) with this range of voice; but its formation for public use lies in our own hands. When we have the good fortune to hear some splendid vocalist, we are apt to think it is simply a gift. Certainly there may be the endowment of a voice capable of great effect; but the singer has not only to learn to play on his instrument, he has, in a sense, to 'make a voice,' and the smoothness, softness, or power to which you listen with delight, is the result of years of study and practice to develop, strengthen, and extend the voice, to obtain perfect command over the breath, and to render the voice, in tone and flexibility, part of himself, and subservient to his will."

After the necessity of making one's self heard, by gaining control over the management of the breath and the production of the series of homogeneous sounds which have been roughly classified in these three registers, careful attention must be devoted to articulation and pronunciation. There must be no slurring and chopping of words, which ought to stand out as clearly defined as "apples of gold in pictures of silver." Words should leave the voice like new coins from the mint—clean cut and clear sounding. There should be no dropping of the final *d* or *g*, such as "an' at" for "an*d* at," or "goin' out" for "goin*g* out;" no "ide*er*" for "idea" (a Cockneyism chargeable to scores of prominent actors); no "f*u*rgiving" when we are "forgiving;" no "vi*e*lence" when "violence" is meant. Space does not here permit the enumeration of one in a hundred of those words which, in the slipshod speech of the drawing-room and the market-place, are seldom properly accentuated or articulated, and often as badly treated on the stage; but the young actor may be advised to pay scrupulous attention to this point, and to articulate each word in accordance with the rules of orthoepy, a knowledge of which is, of course, presupposed.

In endeavouring, however, to produce each word clear cut, and to avoid a liaison between a final consonant and the initial letter of the next word, one must be careful not to fall into the irritating mannerism which is attributed to Macready—that of placing an explosive *a* (or *er*) at the end of certain words, as thus—

"Be innocenttta of knowledge, dearesttta chuck,
Till thou applauddda the deed."

James Murdoch gives an amusing account of Macready's struggle with an American utility actor, who, in announcing the approach of Birnam Wood, insisted on saying—

"Within these three miles you may see it *a*-coming."

"Good heavens, sir!" cried Macready, "have you no ears? You are not speaking common language: it is *blank verse*, sir, and a single misplaced syllable destroys the metre. . . . You know how to spell *coming*, which begins with a *c*—no preceding sound of *a*; therefore you should say—

"'Within these three miles you may see it a-a-coming.'"

The actor tried it over and over again, but could not get rid of the *a*. At last, goaded to despair, he turned upon the tragedian, and said, "Mr. Macready, I don't see the difference between my way of doing it and yours, unless it is that I only put one *a* before 'coming,' and you put half-a-dozen little ones." Macready's reply is not recorded!

It is no excuse for the actor who is guilty of bad articulation that greater than he have made similar errors. Garrick is accused of not giving the letter *a* its full open sound as in "cat," of saying "Isrel" for "Israel," "villin" instead of "villain," and, worse still, "appeal" for "appal." He also talked of "trōpically," "shupreme," and "shuperior." These were the faults of his early days, however, and he is said to have amended them. Quin sounded the *a* in "face" as it should be in "farce," and, with a curious wrongheadedness, sounded "fasces" like "faces," once creating a comical scene by ordering the soldiers in "Coriolanus" to lower their "fa(s)ces," an instruction which they literally obeyed, by bending down their heads! Kemble said "ferse" and "bird" for "fierce" and "beard," his aitches were as variable as the winds, and he is said to have perverted every sound in the language. But though in those famous actors these grievous faults were minimised by their transcendent excellences, they were faults none the less, and as such ought to be avoided by all studious histrions.

Pronunciation varies with the times. What is wrong to-day was correct thirty or forty years ago; what is right to-day may be wrong twenty years hence. During the Augustan era "gold" was "goold," and "china" was "chaney;" and who does not remember Pope's description of Atticus—

> "Dreading e'en fools, by flatterers besieged,
> And so *obleeging* that he ne'er *obleeged*"?

"Obleege" still lingers in parts of Scotland among the vulgar people, but, generally speaking, the mode is now as rare as "Rooshia" for "Russia and "Spaw" for "Spa." Even in our own time pronunciation is changing, con*ténts* and de*táils* are giving place to *cón*tents and *dé*tails; re*vén*ue to *ré*venue; con*tém*plate and il*lús*trate to *cón*template and *íl*lustrate; inter*ést*ing to *ín*teresting; and so on. But it is the actor's duty to inquire as to the correct pronunciation of a word, and to pronounce it as authorities on orthoepy are agreed.

We have now considered the groundwork of all speech; when we pass on to emphasis and pause we arrive at the qualities which give to speech its greatness or its mediocrity. A word can be made to convey just as much, or as little, as the speaker determines; but before he can give the full meaning to a word or sentence, he must himself understand exactly what he desires to convey to the mind of his hearers—the thought must precede and regulate the utterance. "Emphasis and pause," says George Henry Lewes, "are indeed the supreme difficulties of elocution. They are rarely managed by those who read blank verse, even in a room, and on the stage the difficulty is greatly enhanced. Nevertheless, no one can pretend to be an actor of the poetic drama who has not mastered this art; although at the present day it is, like many other requisites, badly disregarded, and we hear the noblest verses spouted (not spoken) with the remorseless indifference of that actor who announced himself thus—

"'Tis I, my lord, the early village cock.'"

Speaking of Kean, the same judicious critic says: "One of his means of effect—sometimes one of his tricks—was to make long pauses between certain phrases. For instance, on quitting the scene, Sir Edward Mortimer has to say warmly, 'Wilford, remember!' Kean used to pause after 'Wilford,' and during the pause his face underwent a rapid succession of expressions, fluently melting into each other, and all tending to one climax of threat; and then the deep tones of 'remember' came like muttered thunder. Those spectators who were unable to catch these expressions considered the pause a mere trick, and sometimes the pauses were only tricks, but often they were subtle truths."

Colley Cibber also touches on the subject of emphasis in these words: "In the just delivery of poetical numbers, particularly where the sentiments are pathetic, it is scarcely credible upon how minute an article of sound depends their greatest beauty or inaffection. The voice of a singer is not more strictly ty'd to time and tune, than that of an actor in theatrical elocution. The least syllable too long, or too slightly dwelt upon in a period, depreciates it to nothing; which very syllable, if rightly touched, shall, like the heightening stroke of light from a master's pencil, give life and spirit to the whole."

It was said that Garrick had not a good ear for emphasis and often misplaced it, a certain 'cute observer pointing out that he said, "And will speak *daggers*, but use *none*; instead of "*Speak* daggers, but *use* none." There seems to have been some truth in the statement;

but Garrick's emphasis must have been correct as a rule, else he could not have become so distinguished an exponent of Shakespeare; for it is by emphasis that the actor illustrates and illuminates the author's words. It is wonderful how much can be conveyed by emphasising one word more than another. As Canon Fleming says: "On the right management of emphasis depends the very spirit and life of good speaking. If no due emphasis is placed on any words, not only is our speaking heavy and lifeless, but there is no intelligent meaning thrown into what we speak or read. Let us take a simple question, 'Do you ride to town to-day?' These six words are capable of no fewer than four different meanings. If pronounced thus, 'Do *you* ride to town to-day?' the answer may be, 'No; I intend to send a messenger in my stead.' If thus, 'Do you *ride* to town to-day?' the answer may be, 'No; I intend to walk.' 'Do you ride to *town* to-day?' 'No; I intend to ride into the country.' 'Do you ride to town *to-day?*' 'No; but I shall do so to-morrow.' Thus, the whole force of an expression may depend on a word, and we may give our hearers quite different views of the same sentence by placing the emphasis differently." In brief, emphasis is the touchstone of speaking; by the relative value placed upon his words we arrive at an estimate of the thoughts passing through the brain of the speaker, and in the case of an actor repeating the words of a poet, we perceive whether or not he has mastered the inner meaning of the lines which the poet puts into his mouth.

"The great difficulty in elocution," says Lewes, "is to be slow, and not to seem slow—to speak the phrases with such distinctness, and such management of the breath, that each shall tell, yet due proportion be maintained. Hurry destroys the effect; and actors hurry, because they dread, and justly dread, the heaviness of a slow utterance. The art is so to manage the time that it shall not appear slow to the hearer; and this is an art very rarely understood by actors. No sooner have they to express excitement, or emotion of any kind, than they seem to lose all mastery over the rhythm and cadence of their speech. Let them study great speakers, and they will find that in passages which seem rapid there is a measured rhythm, and that even in the whirlwind of passion there is as strict a regard to *tempo* as in passionate music. *Resistent flexibility* is the perfection of elocution."

It is a difficult task to strike the golden mean, and while avoiding rant to escape tameness. As Colley Cibber says: "To preserve this medium between mouthing and meaning too little, to keep the attention more pleasingly awake by a tempered spirit than by mere vehemence of voice, is of all the master-strokes of an actor the most difficult to reach." Here no teaching can avail. The discretion of the actor or the speaker must come into play, and it is exactly by the manner in which he brings his own intellectual gifts to bear in preserving this medium that we discriminate between the good actor or the eloquent speaker and the well-drilled "elocutionist."

IV

"SUIT THE ACTION TO THE WORD"

"There was speech in their dumbness, language in their very gesture."—*Winter's Tale*, Act v. sc. 2.

WE now turn to the consideration of one of the most difficult studies connected with the art of acting. It is doubtful if the words from Shakespeare which have been chosen for a heading are sufficient as they stand—"Suit the action to the word"—without those which immediately follow—"the word to the action." For the common mistake of beginners is to take the first six words too literally, and make their actions *follow* their words, failing to notice that they are also enjoined to suit "the word to the action." On second thoughts, however, it will be seen that the phraseology of Shakespeare is studied and carefully worded, so that it should convey to the student a true idea of what is unquestionably the correct and natural thing to do; that, in suiting the action to the word, the word must be suited to the action. That is to say, while the mind of the actor must be in advance of his action and utterance, his action should be in advance of his utterance, *not simultaneous;* so that while he should *mentally* "suit the action to the word," he should really *appear* to suit "the word to the action."

But Shakespeare, well knowing that the vice of all

would-be actors was (and is) excessive gesticulation, makes Hamlet hasten to add, "with this especial observance, that you o'erstep not the modesty of nature; for anything so overdone is *from* the purpose of playing," &c. The great difficulty with the beginner has always been as to which action suits the word, and which word the action, and what may be the modesty of nature. There is some reason for this, too; and generations of schools for "elocution," wherein gesture has been reduced to a few hard and fast mechanical rules, have not done anything to assist the student, but much to hinder him, in arriving at a true estimate of gesture.

The great Betterton, who stands out from all the other figures of the Restoration stage, not only as an actor, but as a man, indulged in very little gesture, being here, again, unlike his contemporaries. We are told that his arms were short and fat, and that he rarely lifted them "higher than his stomach." His left hand was frequently lodged in his breast, between his coat and waistcoat; and with his right he "prepared his speech." This certainly does not convey an idea of suitable gesture; but when we consider that Betterton possessed a somewhat ungainly figure, we can appreciate the good sense of the actor in limiting his gestures to an irreducible minimum and depending upon the power of his eye and the play of his facial expression to illustrate the words he spoke. Moreover, though his gestures were very few, there is no doubt that they were correct and suited to the word, and here we have what is really the secret of good gesticulation—few gestures, but just. Certain it is that Betterton was head and shoulders above all the other players of his time as an artist, and the fact that his effects were obtained with a minimum of physical exertion is important to the student.

Garrick, on the other hand, had a proneness to over-gesticulation, and never quite conquered the art of "repose on the stage." But Garrick's gesture must have been modesty itself compared with the elaborate gesticulation of Quin. We have it, on the authority of "Peregrine Pickle," that Quin in "Zanga" grimaced like a monkey, his delivery of these lines from Zanga's speech regarding the letter being especially ridiculous—

> "He took it up;
> But scarce was it unfolded to his sight
> When he, as if an arrow pierced his eye,
> Started, and trembling dropped it on the ground."

The actor was said to stoop down and seem to pick up something from the stage as he pronounced the first four words; he then mimicked the manner of opening a letter, and the speaking of the third line was accompanied with the darting of his forefinger towards his eye! The word "started" made him recoil with great violence, and he illustrated the remainder of the line by trembling in every limb, and shaking the imaginary letter from his hand. The same absurd idea of suiting the action to the word was observed throughout further portions of Zanga's speech.

It was this chapter in "Peregrine Pickle," descriptive of Quin's prodigality of gesture, that first prompted Macready to tone down his own early excess in the same direction. In one of his letters Macready describes the means whereby he afterwards combated the bad method of gesture which he had formed in his youth. He would lie on the floor, or stand straight against a wall, or tie bandages about his arms, and while so pinioned or restricted, he would recite the most violent passages of "Othello," "Lear," "Hamlet," "Macbeth," or whatever would require most energy and emotion; he would speak the most passionate bursts of rage "under the supposed constraint of whispering them in the ear of him or her to whom they were addressed," thus keeping both voice and gesture in subjection to the real impulse of the feeling. "I was obliged also," he writes, "to have frequent recourse to the looking-glass, and had two or three large ones in my room to reflect to myself each view of the posture I might have fallen into, besides being under the necessity of acting the passion close to a glass to restrain the tendency to exaggerate its expression, which was the most difficult of all, to repress the ready frown, and keep the features, perhaps I should say the muscles of the face, undisturbed, while intense passion should speak from the eye alone. The easier an actor makes his art appear, the greater must have been the pains it cost him."

As Lewes says: "In art simplicity is economy, not meagreness: it is the absence of superfluities, not the suppression of essentials; it arises from an ideal generalisation of real and essential qualities, guided by an exquisite sense of proportion." To quote the same critic again: "All but very great actors are redundant in gesticulation; not simply overdoing the significant, but unable to repress the insignificant movements. . . . If actors will study fine models, they will learn that gestures to be effective must be significant, and to be significant they must be rare."

The student has here a true statement of the standard to which he ought to aspire—to be sparing of gesture, never to make any motion which is not absolutely necessary to assist the spoken word and which is not significant; and, above all, to acquire the art of standing at ease on the stage. But nature is the only guide. An actor who is thoroughly in sympathy with his part, who "feels," as far as it is possible for the actor to feel, the emotions of an imaginary character; such an actor will almost instinctively make correct and natural gestures; for, in so far as he enters into the spirit of his part, he loses that fatal self-consciousness which is the main cause of artificial and redundant gesture. Voltaire understood this perfectly. Preparing a young actress to appear in one of his tragedies, he tied her hands to her sides with pack-thread, in order to check her tendency towards exuberant gesticulation. Under this condition of compulsory immobility she commenced to rehearse, and for some time she bore herself calmly enough; but at last, completely carried away by her feelings, she burst her bonds and flung up her arms. Alarmed at her supposed neglect of his instructions, she began to apologise to the poet; he smilingly reassured her, however; the gesture was *then* admirable, because it was irrepressible.

There are numerous books which pretend to teach the whole art of gesture in so many diagrams, giving the student such priceless information as, "A clenched fist held out and shaken at another person signifies 'rage,' 'anger,' 'passion,'" &c.; or, "The arms outstretched, with the palms of the hands turned outwards, the head looking downward in the opposite direction, signifies 'fear,' 'terror,' 'repugnance,'" &c. Precisely; and when you kick a man on the part of the anatomy usually associated with a kick, that means that you do not love him! All such "guides" to gesture are foolish and futile, and the student who endeavoured to guide his gestures in accordance with their rules and regulations would become about as graceful as the famous

"Purple monkey, climbing on a yellow stick."

Certain methods for walking upon the stage may be imparted to the beginner by some one of experience, but, as Shakespeare says, "let your own discretion be tutor," bearing in mind that the fewer gestures the better—"do not saw the air too much with your hand." The young actor should endeavour to be at his ease, and not to be morbidly conscious of what the audience may be thinking of his every movement. Watch a group of children at play; all their gestures are natural, unaffected, instinct with grace so long as they do not think they are being observed. The actor's art is to be, under the critical gaze of an audience, as natural as those children, to use his hands and arms as he should in speaking with a friend; and that would be rarely, but effectively.

It should also be added that all exercises of the limbs, such as calisthenics, dancing, and fencing, which are designed to impart grace and suppleness to the body, are at the service of the actor, and if he take a course in these his gesticulation will be all the better therefor. A body rendered graceful by means of these physical exercises will be natural in all its movements when controlled by an intelligent mind.

V

THE ART OF MAKING-UP

"MAKING-UP" is one of the most interesting things the actor has to do. The acute observer of humanity must have noticed that every man and woman is animated, more or less, with a desire to look like some one else; nothing gives a youngster so much pleasure as daubing his face with lampblack, and masquerading as a negro; the false-faces which enjoy a brief vogue at Guy Fawkes's Day and Hallowe'en are a source of intense delight to the rising generation; while the unfailing popularity of fancy dress balls and masquerades shows how deep-seated is this desire, even among grown-up people, to appear with a countenance unlike that which greets them every time they consult their mirrors. It is, therefore, only in keeping with the order of things that "making-up" should be one of the most interesting features of the actor's calling, that it should be a task of which the actor never tires; for nothing is more fascinating than to watch an old man's face turning young again, or a young man's face growing old, under the skilful touches of the actor's paints and pencils.

Mr. Cyril Maude, who is an adept in the art of making-up, even in these days when it has been brought to such perfection, testifies, in another page of this book, to the great pleasure he derives from this part of his work, and says it generally takes him an hour to change himself into one of the old men he impersonates with so much artistic finish. Mr. Beerbohm Tree is also noted for the wonderful effects he has obtained in this direction, his make-up in Falstaff being a veritable triumph of disguise; and while the more striking personality of Sir Henry Irving is less capable of complete disguise, who has not marvelled at the remarkable manner in which he has changed that scores of times, from Jeremy Diddler to King Lear, and the wondrous perfection of detail which marks all he does?

In the classical theatre there was no attempt at "make-up," unless we might regard the masks which the actors wore as a primitive form of disguise. But these masks were so utterly unlike anything in nature that their use was antagonistic to the very idea of making-up, which aims at realising in the appearance of the actor the physical attributes of the character he is impersonating. From the earliest beginnings of acting in England some endeavour had been made to change the appearance of the actor by treatment of the face, either with paints or beards, though not until the earlier years of the present century was this done with such regard to the character to be represented that it could be looked upon as a valuable adjunct of the actor's art. Shakespeare makes Bottom, the Weaver, greatly exercised in his mind as to his make-up for Pyramus. "What beard were I best to play it in?" asks he who offered to roar the Lion's part as gently as any sucking-dove. "I will discharge it in either your straw-coloured beard, your orange-tawny beard, your purple-in-grain beard, or your French-crown-colour beard, your perfect yellow." The beard was evidently an important item of the make-up at this time, and Bottom's readiness to don one of any colour is, no doubt, Shakespeare's way of hinting at the lack of suitability which characterised the actors' make-up at that time.

Johnson, an actor of the Restoration stage, seems to have developed the art of making-up to an extent which Downes, the author of "Roscius Anglicanus," thought worthy of mention; for that curious old author, who was prompter at Lincoln's Inn Fields theatre from 1662 to 1706, says of him that he was "skilful in the art of painting, which is a great adjument very promovent to the art of elocution." Johnson was an exception, however, as Waldron, who annotated a new edition of "Roscius Anglicanus" in 1789, says that the painting of the face and marking it with dark lines to imitate the wrinkles of old age "was formerly carried to excess on the stage, though now a great deal disused. I have seen actors (he continues) who were really older than the characters they were to represent, mark their faces with black lines of Indian ink to such a degree that they appeared as if looking through a mask of wire." Waldron also mentions Garrick's "skill in the necessary preparation of his face for the aged and venerable Lear, and for Lusignan," which, he says, "was as remarkable as his performance of those characters was admirable." But there is reason to believe that Garrick relied more on his wonderful powers of facial expression than upon the artificial, but invaluable, aid of the "make-up box."

Colley Cibber says of Dogget, the celebrated comedian of Queen Anne's time, that he was remarkably skilful "in dressing a character to the greatest exactness. . . . The least article of whatever habit he wore seemed to speak and mark the different humour he represented; a necessary care in a comedian, in which many have been too remiss or ignorant." Another contemporary writer says that Dogget "could, with the greatest exactness, paint his face so as to represent the ages of seventy, eighty, and ninety distinctly, which occasioned Sir Godfrey Kneller to tell him one day at Button's Coffee-house, that he excelled him in painting, for that he could only paint from the originals before him, but that he (Dogget) could vary them at pleasure, and yet keep a close likeness." In the character of Moneytrap, the Miser, in Vanbrugh's comedy of "The Confederacy," Dogget is described as wearing "an old threadbare black coat, to which he had put new cuffs, pocket-lids, and buttons, on purpose to make its rusticness more conspicuous. The neck was stuffed so as to make him appear round-shouldered, and give his head the greater prominence; his squared-toed shoes were large enough to buckle over those he wore in common, which made his legs appear much smaller than usual." All these facts indicate that, with the care of a thorough artist, Dogget neglected no detail which might tend to heighten the effect of his impersonation.

But it is a work of supererogation to argue by illustration, or otherwise, the necessity of the actor spending care and thought on the art of making-up. It is almost as essential that the actor should *look* his part, as that he should *act* it. In another chapter the question of dress is considered, and here we are only concerned with the face and head; but it is the face and head that give the index to character. To this end a knowledge of physiognomy ought to be acquired; that is, the physiognomy of life, not of the stage, according to the foolish traditions of which a villain should always have black hair, a hero or heroine flaxen locks, and a humorous character a red wig. These are traditions which still linger on the boards for no intelligent reason, as black hair is not a necessary badge of villainy, nor are golden curls the *sine quâ non* of virtue, or a carroty wig the cause or effect of comicality or stupidity—for it is used, oddly enough, to represent both. The young actor should study these things for himself, and preferably from originals. Let him select the living type of character he wishes to portray and arrange his make-up accordingly.

There are many books which purport to give instruction in this connection; but it is doubtful if direct advice can be of any great assistance, further than in specifying the materials used for obtaining certain effects. Experience and an artistic eye will enable the actor to so make up his face that, though he is only twenty years of age, his complexion may be sixty or seventy; or he may, when in the sere and yellow leaf, be able, as many have been before, to play juvenile characters with a countenance that might have seen no more than twenty summers. One thing should always be borne in mind, however, and that is, that the actor's face must not be made up to look correct at a few paces. It requires to be so marked that in the unnatural glare of the footlights it may seem natural. To attain this end constant observation of others is necessary, for one actor cannot so experiment on himself; and no general rule can be framed for his guidance in this mattter. It is a want of regard for this important point, or an ignorance of how to obtain a proper effect, that makes so many of the faces we see on the stage to-day, especially among actresses, like nothing so much as Lowther Arcadian dolls.

Miss Helen Faucit (Lady Martin) says a few words on the mistake of overpainting, which should receive careful attention: "The abuse of cosmetics on the French stage," she writes, "which was then (1845) habitual, has since been carried in many instances to excess upon our own. When the skin is covered with what is, in fact, a painted mask, the colour, which under strong emotion would come and go, is hidden under it, and the natural expression of the countenance destroyed." The justice of this is obvious. To besmear the face with paint is really to cover it almost as effectually as some actors have hidden the faces of their Othellos in crape masks, thus killing all the effect which should be produced in the complexion of the face by the passing emotions—such as the blush of modesty or indignation, the flush of anger or excitement, and the pallor of terror or rage.

In one old authority on the art of making-up, quoted by Dutton Cook, the importance of rouge is set forth, with the manner of applying it by means of a hare's foot. It should not be too manifest, yet "it should be placed well under the eyes, to impart to them a brilliant, sparkling appearance." Pearl powder is also recommended to whiten the forehead, neck, arms, and hands. The facetious uses of rouge are also dwelt upon. "If a comic face be wanted, the rouge should be placed on the tip of the nose or down it in a streak, also laid on the cheek bones or across the forehead. This, however, must not be overdone." There must be reason even in rouging. The actor is then advised that when he would remove paint from his cuticle, he should not attempt to wash it off, but should simply smear cold cream over his face: afterwards with a dry towel he will be able to wipe off cold cream and colour both. He is then told how to impart to youth the aspect of age, with the help of sepia or Indian-ink and a camel's-hair brush. The lines running down the nose, the furrows across the forehead, the crow's-feet about the eyes, and the lines round the mouth and chin, are to be deepened and refined by the paint-brush. White and sepia are to be employed when a sick or emaciated appearance is thought necessary, and when a "bald wig" is assumed the better to portray age, care is to be taken to colour the natural skin of the forehead to match the hue of the artificial skin or canvas scalp of the wig.

In M. Gustave Garcia's treatise on the actor's art, the student is very properly advised to study the works of the painters to gain some idea of the general effects which should be aimed at in making up the face; and M. Garcia says, with a reason which does not distinguish all his advice: "We may assert that if an actor is fully penetrated with his part he will require but very few touches to complete a picture, which his action, words, and attitudes already greatly contribute to represent." He also gives the following very useful hints to assist the student in his or her experiments:—

Pearl white, rouge, and violet powder are the principal ingredients used to make up a young face, and are applied in the following manner:—If the complexion is fair, simply spread some cold cream on the face, and with a puff put some violet powder or powdered magnesia. If the skin is dark, it is necessary to mix some pearl white with cold cream and spread it carefully, so as not to leave any patches. As this mineral white is crude in shade, it is desirable to soften it by passing violet powder over it, thus giving transparency to the complexion. The application of the rouge must begin immediately under the eyelashes and spread mostly on the bony part of the cheek, leaving the nose untouched. Want of discrimination in the use of rouge would cause the face to look like a highly-coloured doll; this would not harmonise with the natural complexion. The rouge and white must blend together. A thin line of dark brown traced over the lower eyelashes gives force of expression and brightness to the eyes.

For an African complexion, we should take amber brown, mixed with the smallest quantity of purple brown; this made into a very thin paste with cold cream or lard, would be a near approach to an African complexion. Care must be taken in all cases to spread over the colouring a dry powder of the same colour, mixed with a small quantity of magnesia or violet powder, so as to counteract the shiny appearance caused by the use of cold cream.

Ochre, mixed with a very small quantity of amber brown, would imitate a sallow complexion, such as we often see in old people.

Amber brown, mixed with a smaller quantity of chrome, and the smallest possible quantity of purple brown, would imitate the dull colour of a Persian.

Wrinkles are traced or imitated by means of paste pencils, such as are to be had at theatrical hairdressers. Pure black is too crude and hard for this purpose, as it gives an unnatural appearance and makes up what we call a "dirty" face. The colours must be as nearly as possible an approach to the natural colour of the skin. The actor must trace with the pencils the lines of the face, round the eyes, alongside the nose, and on the forehead, having previously spread a very thin coating of cold cream all over the face.

The eyebrows are whitened with pearl white (*blanc de perle*) mixed with cold cream. Violet powder or magnesia spread over the face, with or without any of the powders above mentioned, will blend all the colours together, and tone down the general make-up.

A bald wig requires a great deal of attention so as to look natural, as the colour given to it by the hairdresser rarely corresponds to that of our complexion. The line caused by the wig on the forehead is also very offensive to the eye. In order to avoid these contrasts it is necessary to spread a flesh-coloured pomatum on the wig and forehead, so as to blend the two together.

We recommend cold cream instead of water for the mixing of colours; not only does it spread evenly on the face without patches, but the perspiration does not affect it, nor does the skin get so easily injured. Magnesia is an excellent substitute for violet powder—easy to get, cheaper, and free from chalk. A thin coating of amber brown, mixed with a very small quantity of white, and spread under the eyes, gives them a sunken appearance.

Chrome and violet powder mixed together deaden the colour of the skin and give a ghastly appearance. The same mixture can be made into a paste. When the eyes have a sunken appearance, rouge on the nose, and a very little on the bony part of the cheek, with chrome mixed with white spread over the face, gives the appearance of a low, drunken type.

A thin coating of amber brown, spread in the hollow of the cheeks, will make the face look thinner.

The combination of the eyes and cheeks being sunk, a thin coating of chrome mixed with white powder over the face will give the appearance of a dying person. In this case no rouge should be used.

A little crimson paste on the lips, as well as a little rouge on the tips of the ears, and also on the nails, will add freshness and transparency to the skin. Care must be taken to whiten the neck and hands.

There are many ways of making up the face that are more or less typical, and which words cannot possibly describe. It is for the actor to study the combination of colours and general effect, so as to *look* the part he has to play.

It is said that the celebrated French actress, Dejazet, who played the parts of young lovers at the age of seventy, used to get rid of her numerous wrinkles by means of elastic wigs that kept the skin tightly drawn from the forehead.

The wig, of course, is a most important item of the player's make-up; and so much has the art of the theatrical *coiffeur* been developed, that nowadays it may be said there is absolutely no type of humanity which cannot be represented by means of specially-constructed wigs. An actor with a thick crop of hair can appear as an old gentleman with a head as bare and shiny as a billiard ball; a low forehead can be made as high and domelike as Shakespeare's or Sir Walter Scott's, or a high one made to appear as low as Bill Syke's; a pugnose may be made as perfect as a Grecian by means of papier-mâché; hollow cheeks, by a similar device, can be made to rival those of the Fat Boy; while chubby cheeks, by a skilful application of amber brown, will become as lean and withered as a pantaloon's. But enough has been said on this subject to indicate its importance to the stage student; though it is impossible, in the compass of a few pages, to do more than touch it suggestively.

VI

CONCERNING COSTUME

NOWADAYS there are no two opinions as to the value—nay, the necessity—of correct costumes upon the stage. Time was, and that not so long ago in the history of the Drama, when the greatest actors of the day thought fit to appear before their audiences in dresses that had no more association with the characters they assumed than there is likeness between the attire of the present day Piccadilly fop and that of John the Baptist. Indeed, one reads with a feeling akin to amazement, of the ridiculous guises with which actors of the fame of Betterton and Garrick were wont to furnish their characters. The first-named genius played Hamlet in the English dress of his own period, wearing the laced kerchief then in fashion; and we are told that his face blanched as white as his neckcloth at the appearance of the ghost, an accomplishment that, in some degree, made up for the unsuitability of the dress. Garrick's Hamlet was apparelled in a court suit of black—a coat, waistcoat, and knee breeches, short wig with queue and bag, buckles on the shoes, ruffles at the wrists, and the flowing ends of an ample cravat hanging over the chest. It would be no more absurd for Sir Henry Irving to play the melancholy Dane in an evening dress and an opera hat.

Although Garrick was the innovator of many much-needed reforms during his famous reign at the national temple of the drama, there is no evidence that he ever made any real attempt to dress his productions with more regard than was then manifested on the stage to the manners and customs of the times which they were supposed to represent. His Othello was a failure mainly on account of his own physical unfitness, and his dressing the noble Moor more after the style of a negro flunkey than like the mighty master of many legions. He restored the original text of "Macbeth" to the stage, but he played the Thane of Cawdor in an officer's scarlet coat, a waistcoat laced with silver, with a wig, and breeches of the cut then in fashion! Zoffany's picture of the dagger scene shows him in this dress, and that of Dawes depicts him in the fighting scene dressed as a *Spanish* general, with breastplate, slashed trunks, large pointed hat, and open collar! His Hotspur wore a laced frock and a Ramillies tye-wig. A tye-wig was also part of the "get-up" of the ghost in "Macbeth," and a sagacious critic wrote to Garrick pointing out the absurdity of this, in view of the line addressed to the apparition—

> "Why dost thou shake thy *gory locks?*"

But the same critic only found fault with Garrick's own dress on the ground that it was *too insignificant* for Macbeth, and ought to have been laced with gold instead of silver.

When the apostle of the "life" school made no serious attempt to clothe his characters with any approach to historical accuracy, it is not surprising to learn that those of his contemporaries, who were declaimers rather than impersonators, were completely negligent in the matter of costume. At the age of sixty Quin played

Chamont, a young Bohemian nobleman of a remote romantic period, "in a long grisly, half-powdered wig, hanging low down on each side of the breast, and down the back; a heavy scarlet coat and waistcoat, trimmed with broad gold lace, black velvet breeches, a black silk neckcloth, black stockings, a pair of square-toed shoes, with an old-fashioned pair of stone buckles, and a pair of stiff high-topped white gloves, with a broad old scolloped hat." But John Kemble was as bad, if not, in some respects, worse than his immediate predecessors in his ideas of suitable costumes. His Hamlet was dressed in "a fancy suit which defied chronology, a carefully curled and powdered wig, such as never sat on Scandinavian head, and a blaze of jewelled orders—on the breast of him who courted seclusion." How sadly his ideas of propriety must have been astray is seen in the fact that in his earlier appearances as Hamlet Kemble actually wore the Order of the Garter beneath his knee, and he appeared in the mad scene wearing the ribbon and star, with a black velvet court dress, diamond buckles, and his powdered hair dishevelled. Could anachronism go further? Yes, it could, and Kemble himself proved it, as he took part in a play of the period of the Norman Conquest wearing the Order of the Elephant, which was not instituted till the middle of the fifteenth century! And in Hotspur he wore the Order of the Garter—he had evidently a weakness for "Orders"—even after proof was shown that young Percy had never been a member of the Order.

Fitful efforts had been made in the seventeenth century to present a play dressed with some consideration of the period in which its action took place; but in the eighteenth century, and, as we have seen, despite the advent of the great reformer Garrick, there seems to have been no more lasting efforts at appropriate dressing, the one idea of actors and actresses being to strut about in the most gorgeous raiment they could afford to purchase, no matter whether their vestments were in keeping with their parts or not. And yet, such attempts as were made, Macklin's Shylock, for instance, always appear to have met with approval, showing that the audiences would have welcomed a change in the proper direction if the actors had cared to make it. Well on into the present century there had been little or no improvement in the matter of which we write; and though Edmund Kean introduced many improvements, even he was not always accurate in his dress, while Macready occasionally made mistakes that almost seem impossible in one who had been such a diligent and intelligent student of dramatic and general literature. Gautier ridicules his dress in Othello as grotesque, and Mr. John Coleman, who was present when Forrest hissed Macready in Edinburgh, gives the following sketch of his Hamlet costume on that occasion:—"He wore a dress, the waist of which nearly reached his arms; a hat with a sable plume big enough to cover a hearse; a pair of black silk gloves much too large for him: a ballet skirt of straw-coloured satin, which looked simply dirty; and what with his gaunt, awkward, angular figure, his grizzled hair, his dark beard close shaven to his square jaws, yet unsoftened by a trace of pigment, his irregular features, his queer, extraordinary nose, . . . and his long skinny neck, he appeared positively hideous. But, after all, 'mind is the brightness of the body,' and, O ye gods! when he spoke, how he brightened, illumined, irradiated the atmosphere."

Broadly speaking, there has been a continual improvement in stage costume these last fifty years, Charles Kean's and Phelps's elaborate Shakespearian productions having done much to spread the taste for appropriate dress; but it may be fairly said that the present generation of players is the first in which a general observance of historical fashions has characterised stage costumery.

Even to-day we have not reached all-round perfection, as we often see an actor going through two or three scenes without a change of dress in circumstances which should have suggested an alteration, or appearing after the supposed lapse of years in a garb he had worn in the first act; while it is no uncommon thing, especially in melodrama, to see a poor starving heroine, huddled in a corner of the stage with the pitiless paper snow falling upon her high-heeled, patent leather shoes, and her bejewelled fingers glistening among her picturesque rags. But, on the whole, there is a commendable attention paid nowadays to appropriate costume, the example set by Sir Henry Irving and others having largely brought about the general excellence.

There are no hard and fast rules, of course, to be laid down for the guidance of the actor with regard to dress. His own sense of propriety and suitability must be his guide. Where the character to be impersonated belongs to a definite historical era there are the researches of the historian to assist the actor, who should ransack every accessible authority that may enable him to arrive at a proper idea of the dress which the character he is to impersonate would have worn in real life. And where the part is one in which a type of character is to be portrayed in a modern play there is an abundance of living models to study in the teeming life around us, peculiarities of face and dress to be noted, copied, and, perhaps, delicately exaggerated upon the stage. It is entirely a question of suitability. As Sir Henry Irving says: "Suitability is demanded in all things; and it must, for instance, be apparent to all, that the things suitable to a palace are different to those usual in a hovel. There is nothing unsuitable in Lear in kingly raiment in the hovel in the storm, because such is here demanded by the exigencies of the play; but if Lear were to be first shown in such guise in such a place with no explanation given of the cause, either the character or the stage-manager would simply be taken for a madman."

Audiences are so much better educated nowadays than they were in Garrick's time, and in the earlier years of the century, that the actor who dared to disregard an approximation to historical accuracy in his dress would speedily be reminded of the fact. But the actor of to-day who did anything of the kind would not be entitled to credit as an artist; for on the stage nothing should be despised which is calculated to better enable the audience to realise the truth of the picture, and in this light the question of costume is one of immense importance.

VII

STAGE TRADITIONS

ONE of the first things the young actor finds himself confronted with is the dead wall of "stage tradition." When he gets his first important character, provided it is in an old play, he will be told by some "old stager" that the great Mr. So-and-so did this or that in such and such a place, that he wore a red wig with three hairs sticking down on his noble brow, and his left shoe only half buckled. And because the great Mr. So-and-so did these wonderful things so must the budding Mr. Beginner, though a generation intervene. It is to be feared that even in these days, when stage traditions are "more honoured in the breach than the observance," there are many of the older actors who look askance on any new claimant for dramatic honours who dares to disregard the wisdom of the ancients and present a character in accordance with his own conception and not on the lines which some actor of a past generation had conceived to be correct. Yet, on the whole, there is much encouragement nowadays for the innovator, for is not everything "new" especially favoured just now—the "new humour," the "new fiction," the "new criticism," and—shall we say?—the "new acting." Indeed, the young actor must be careful that in evading the Scylla of tradition he is not sucked into the Charybdis of *bizarrerie*. For an obvious striving after new "effects" is as undesirable as the staginess which results from too much respect for tradition.

There is nothing more at variance with a true conception of the art of acting than that an actor should be expected to do certain things for no better reason than that some one more famous than himself had done them many years before. To this day, the Théâtre Français is, to some extent, a treasure-house—or lumber room—of tradition, and contemporary French acting is largely based on the acting of previous generations. It is only within the present century that English acting may be said to have broken away from the bonds of a dead past, to have thrown off the yoke of tradition. Up to the time of Garrick no actor of an heroic part would have dreamt of facing an audience without his enormous plume of feathers, which was thought to import dignity, while tragedy would have been impossible had the actors worn socks instead of buskins, although it is difficult to understand how the covering of the feet affected the emotions of the heart. Garrick himself, while he rode rough-shod through many conventionalities of the stage, also retained many, and even created others. He used the two miniatures in "Hamlet," in the scene with the Queen, at the passage, "Look upon this picture, and on this;" and when Henderson, who was one of his immediate successors, ventured to "improve" the point by throwing away the portrait of Hamlet's uncle after the odious comparison, Garrick's admirers found fault with the new actor, because, forsooth, the great Garrick had not done so! Henderson, anxious to please the drama's patrons, retained the miniature in his hand the next time, and was then ridiculed by the Garrick faction on the ground that if he was right the first time he was necessarily wrong the *second!* The same critics condemned the same actor because he did not manage his hat "properly"—that is to say, as Garrick did—on seeing the Ghost; while he placed himself beyond the pale of their esteem on account of his omitting to upset the chair in his agitation—as Garrick had done, having the legs so bent inwards that the chair toppled over on the slightest touch. Garrick himself adhered to the old custom of drawing his sword when Horatio wished to detain him from following the Ghost, but on the latter saying, "I am thy father's spirit," he, with a respectful bow, put up his weapon, as if he would not have sheathed it had the disembodied spirit belonged to any one else!

Probably one of the reasons why Garrick abolished the gravediggers from his perversion of "Hamlet" was because these characters, as played by the clowns of the time, were absurdly burlesqued, the first grave-digger obtaining his greatest effect by divesting himself of half-a-dozen different waistcoats, a piece of buffoonery which survived till 1831, when Leigh Hunt expressed his pleasure at its abolition. Even in 1838, when Compton played the part to Charles Kean's Prince at Drury Lane, his refusal to play to the gallery in this piece of worthless buffoonery was specially noted by Bunn as an admirable innovation; while Charles Kean's discarding of the vulgarism, which Macready and many of the earlier Hamlets resorted to, in order to represent the distemper of Hamlet's mind—appearing with one stocking "fouled, ungartered, and downgyved to his ankle"—was also applauded by the same critic. The robbing the gravedigger of his waistcoats was a reform that even had its opponents among the would-be critical, and one such pointed out to Leigh Hunt that, as the practice had been observed since Shakespeare's day, it was most likely that Shakespeare approved of it. Because it was done in Shakespeare's day did not, of course, signify that the poet approved it any more than it constituted the practice right and proper. There are many things done by actors which their authors by no means favour, but which they cannot control; and it betrays a rather poor conception of Shakespeare's genius to suppose he could ever have been party to such paltry fooling.

For many years it was customary for the face of the First Murderer in "Macbeth" to be thickly chalked, and this, contrasted with a heavy black wig and black whiskers, was supposed to make him ghastly. This was done in Garrick's day and later. Then, in Otway's touching play, "Venice Preserved," the ghosts of Pierre and Jaffier used to appear in tangible shape to Belvidera. Garrick observed this custom, and it was left for Barry, many years later, to abolish the apparitions and make them appear to the mind's eye of Belvidera; a plan which should be followed whenever possible, as the introduction of a ghost is always a matter of difficulty, and stage ghosts have a habit of appearing anything but ethereal. In this same play, when Pierre addressed the conspirators—"Or thou! with that lean withered face!"—it was the custom for a ghastly, shrunken object to come forward and excite the derision of the audience. Even to-day we have not quite got rid of the grotesque figure of the Apothecary in "Romeo and Juliet." He used to be made up like a pantomime caricature, and to-day his poverty is generally overdone to the point of burlesque. Such traditions die hard.

These facts have been recapitulated merely to illustrate how strong a hold a tradition may secure, and many more might be adduced; such as the absurd cock-crowing which used to be introduced in "Hamlet," so that the Ghost might have some obvious cause for starting "like a guilty thing upon a fearful summons."

This actually obtained in Garrick's time; while it is a commonplace of stage history that Shylock was a red-headed, whimsical Jew until Macklin's historical performance, and, in a modified way, till Kean's great impersonation made such a monstrosity impossible. Polonius, too, is not yet entirely free from the suspicion of his former comical days, when that character was the especial preserve of humorous actors.

There are, of course, traditions which are of value to the actor if the character he is to impersonate is one which, like those of Shakespeare, has held the stage for generations; but it is the duty of the modern actor to examine the traditions clustering round the part he may be studying, and if these do not appeal to his sense of what is right and proper, to reject them without compunction.

The great error generally made by those whose respect for traditional methods and stage conventionalities colours the whole of their acting, is to mistake mannerisms for art, faults or peculiarities for excellences; indeed, many of the most dearly cherished traditions have been nothing more or less than the merest oddities of this great actor or that, in repeating which men of lesser talent have laid the flattering unction to their soul that they were doing something which was bound to be good, simply because the great Mr. So-and-so did it. The faults of great actors are always the easiest things to imitate, and that is why they are so frequently reproduced, but when an inferior actor, through want of thought and discrimination, copies the faults of a greater he only does himself harm, in that he gives his audience faults for his best, whereas these faults in the greater actor were counterbalanced by native excellences which his imitator does not possess. "Traditions," Sir Henry Irving says, "are often good; but though excellent for those who invented them, they are often singularly bad for those who try to carry them on."

Broadly speaking, it may be affirmed that the young actor should beware of tradition, and never do anything that some veteran would have him do, "because Mr. Blank always did so, you know." He must *think* for himself, and if his acting be guided by thought, and not by rote, he will be able to determine, first, whether this action, or "point," of Mr. Blank's is really worthy of a conscientious artist, whether it is a fault or a beauty; and secondly, whether it is suited to himself, and might with advantage be reproduced. But for tradition *as such* there should be scant regard. Those whose acting is guided by what actors of the past were wont to do are like the Chinese who worship their ancestors, and the art which lives on the art of the past is as akin to true art as the Tierra del Fuegian, who eats his grandmother, is to civilisation.

VIII

ACTOR AND AUDIENCE

BETWEEN the actor and his audience a subtle sympathy must exist, or else the audience will never be touched by the work of the actor. His art may be worthy of much critical laudation, but if it lack that "soul," which all the rules, regulations, and maxims in the world will not supply if it be not present in the actor himself, it will not touch the heart of his audience; it will not, as Mrs. Kendal very aptly says, "go over the footlights." That is why there are many people who are correctly said to be "good actors," their knowledge of stage-craft, capacity for easy utterance, graceful gesture and becoming action, being indisputable; but yet they lack this "sympathy," "soul," "genius"—call it what you may—that enables other players, less excellent, perhaps, in details, to reach the hearts of their audience. The first quality "to move men's hearts" is earnestness; the importance of being earnest should be impressed on every student, for if he is earnest himself the actor has taken the first step towards convincing his audience. But even those whose temperaments do not enable them to get inside their characters, forcing them to stand outside, as it were, using the acknowledged symbols of their art to express emotions which they are unable themselves to thoroughly realise; even such soulless actors (if the epithet can be used without implying complete condemnation) may not find it impossible to win the esteem and respect, if not the love and admiration, of the audience, provided they zealously strive to please, and scrupulously guard against any action, look, or bearing on the stage which might place them completely out of sympathy with their audience.

There are some would-be geniuses who would have us suppose that the audience is a small consideration with them; but the actor who says that he never concerns himself with what the audience may think of his performances, is either a knave or a fool—and more probably the one than the other. It is the laudable ambition of every actor to win the approval of his audience; and the actor owes a duty to his audience as well as to his author, although, in discharging the latter, he largely fulfils the former. All honest actors readily admit the stimulus derived from the applause of the audience. Mr. Toole, in the preface to his "Reminiscences," touches on the subject very happily. The favourite comedian says: "I am occasionally called upon to make a speech in public. Well, I get along now and then pretty well, thanks to the inspiration that seems to come to me from the friendly sympathy of my audience; but there is no inspiration in a blank sheet of paper, and there is no applause in pens and ink. When one makes a speech one sees kindly faces around one, and it is wonderful what assistance there is in a little applause. You take up the report of a speech in a newspaper; you see that it is peppered with 'laughter,' 'applause,' 'loud cheers,' and so on; that sets you reading it, and carries you on to the end. It is very much the same with a speaker; he makes his little joke, and there is a laugh, which helps him to his next; then he says a nice thing about the occasion, and gets a round of applause; that helps him on his road to the climax, when he hopes to finish up, and mostly does, with a burst of enthusiasm. What I am coming to is an emphasis of my original point—the tremendous difference between speaking and writing." And Mr. Toole proceeds to reaffirm his opinion as to the immense stimulus which the actor, or the orator, receives from the applause of his audience.

Mrs. Kendal touching this point says: "If an audience is very attentive to a play, they get the very best that an artist can give them; whilst, on the contrary, if you feel the public are not with you, you become self-conscious and can do nothing. One's feeling of the audience is more a general impression than noticing particular persons. Sometimes one notices more, sometimes less. The only people that I can see in a theatre are those who are very near to me—the people in the first row or two of the stalls, and the people in the private boxes. I always feel very conscious of them, because they seem to be so near, but otherwise one can have no judgment of the effect one is producing, because one cannot see—at least, there are only a very few people with long sight who can see all over the house. But you can instinctively *feel* whether the people are listening to you or whether you are gaining their attention."

There is not the slightest doubt that the conscientious artist is, as he certainly ought to be, always thoughtful of his audience: for, after all, the audience is the first and final court to which the actor must make his appeal. Kean's whole-souled devotion to his art in his earlier days will not be called in question, and it was during these days that he was most exercised in his mind as to how he might win the approval of his audience. It was only in his later years, during his decline, that he occasionally forgot the duty he owed to those who had paid their money to see him act his very best. Once when he was playing at Exeter in his strolling days, "My fortune is made," exclaimed he, in an ecstatic manner to a friend; "Lord and Lady Cork are coming to see my Othello to-morrow night, and Lord Cork is esteemed a very good judge of acting, as you know." The discrimination exhibited by my Lord Cork on the night referred to scarcely justified his reputation as "a very good judge of acting." "Well, Kean, what success?" asked his friend on the following day. "Oh, sir," returned the tragedian, "don't mention it; I'm miserable. While I was playing the finest parts of Othello in my best style, Lord and Lady Cork's children were playing at hot cockles in front of the box, and my Lord and Lady Cork laughing at them." This raises the other question, namely, the duty of the audience to the actor; but that may be dismissed by saying that, as a general rule, the audience is the more dutiful of the two. The actor who "gags," who is careless in his make-up, who does not trouble to speak so that his voice may be heard in every part of the house, is at once disloyal to his art, his author, and his audience; and the pity is that there are many such.

Another instance of Kean's anxiety to please his audience in his best days is worthy of record. On the occasion of his first performance of Sir Giles Overreach, the intensity of his acting was such that we are told "scream after scream reverberated through the solemn stillness of the house—a silence now broken by the confusion caused by the removal of hysterical women; Lord Byron was seized with a sort of convulsive fit; the pit rose *en masse;* all parts of the house followed its example; and as hats and handkerchiefs were waved with unparalleled enthusiasm, thunders on thunders of applause swept over the theatre." When Kean went home from this great performance his wife—who would have been a suitable companion for Garrick in that she "dearly loved a lord"—asked, "Well, Edmund, and what did Lord Essex say of it?" "Damn Lord Essex, Mary," retorted the tragedian with impulsive contempt; and then with enthusiasm, "the pit rose at me!"

Self-consciousness, as has already been remarked, is the secret of failure to get *en rapport* with one's audience. It sometimes leads to more disastrous results. Dutton Cook tells the tragic story of Adolphe Nourritt, who had been the chief tenor at the Paris Opera House for sixteen years. He had "created" the leading characters in "Robert," "Les Huguenots," "La Juive," "Gustave," and "Masaniello." He resigned his position precipitately upon the advent of Duprez. The younger singer afflicted the elder with a kind of panic. The news that Duprez was among his audience was sufficient to paralyse his powers, to extinguish his voice. He left France for Italy. His success was unquestionable, but he had lost confidence in himself; a deep dejection settled upon him, his apprehension of failure approached delirium. At last he persuaded himself that the applause he won from a Neapolitan audience was purely ironical, was but scoffing ill-disguised. At five in the morning, on the 8th of March 1839, he flung himself from the window of an upper floor, and was picked up in the street quite dead. This is an instance of a great singer, and one not without a touch of genius, being more concerned about his personal success over a rival than the art he practised. Had Nourritt been a thorough artist, devoted to his art for his art's sake, and not to himself, this morbid self-consciousness, which led to his suicide, could not have gained the mastery.

Much might be written on this subject, but the duties

which the actor owes to his audience are really the duties he owes to his art. His great aim is to make the audience believe that he believes, and to this end all obvious stage-tricks should be avoided like poison, as on their detection by the audience the necessary illusion is destroyed, the object of the actor's art is unattained.

Madame Malibran is reported to have said that her method of acquiring ease when before an audience was to imagine she was singing in a garden, and the audience represented so many heads of cabbage. From this it would appear the prima donna's opinion of her audience was not particularly flattering, and it betrays a peculiar idea of art; for the vocalist who could sing better to a plot of vegetable marrows than to an audience pulsing with the blood of life and human sympathy, would seem to be awanting in this last quality herself. But, apart from that, it is the height of folly to say that any one could be such an ineffable fool as to suppose his or her audience to be a collection of cabbages; and even if the actor could so force his soul to that conceit, it is difficult to distinguish wherein the advantage should lie—whether it would be better for him to feel that his words were falling on the ears of actual human beings, and sinking into human souls, or that they were falling upon the unreceptive leaves of cabbages which might be used for to-morrow's soup!

Rather should these glowing words of Sir Henry Irving be commended to the attention of the student: "How noble the privilege to work upon these finer—these finest—feelings of universal humanity. How engrossing the fascination of these thousands of steady eyes, and sound sympathies, and beating hearts which an actor confronts, with the confidence of friendship and co-operation, as he steps upon the stage to work out in action his long-pent comprehension of a noble masterpiece! How rapturous the satisfaction of abandoning himself in such a presence, and with such sympathisers, to his author's grandest flights of thought and noblest bursts of emotional inspiration! And how perpetually sustaining the knowledge that whatever may be the vicissitudes and even the degradations of the stage, it must and will depend for its constant hold on the affection and attention of mankind upon its loftier work; upon its more penetrating passion; upon its themes which most deeply search out the strong affections and high hopes of men and women; upon its fit and kindling illustration of great and vivid lives which either have been lived in noble fact, or have deserved to endure immortally in the popular belief and admiration which they have secured!"

PART II

THREE GREAT ACTORS

THEIR LIVES AND OPINIONS

I

DAVID GARRICK

"If manly sense; if nature linked with art;
If thorough knowledge of the human heart;
If powers of acting, vast and unconfined;
If fervent faults with greatest beauties joined;
If strong expression and strange pow'rs which lie
Within the magic circle of the eye;
If feelings which few hearts like his can know,
And which no face so well as *his* can show,
Deserve the preference—Garrick, take the chair,
Nor quit it till thou place an equal there."

—*The Rosciad.*

THESE lines, from Churchill's famous satire, rather than the foolish bombast under Garrick's statue in Westminster Abbey—

"Shakespeare and Garrick like twin stars shall shine,
And earth irradiate with a beam divine,

which excited the disgust of Charles Lamb, and tempted him to write his somewhat ill-judged essay on "The Tragedies of Shakespeare considered with reference to their fitness for Stage Representation," seem to best sum up the famous actor whose life and work we are about to consider.

In writing of an actor it is always necessary to glance, however briefly, at his earlier life—his boyhood and adolescence; for in an actor, even more than in the follower of any other art, these years are significant, and therefore worthy of examination. The influence of juvenile surroundings generally bears more pronouncedly on the after career of the actor than on that of any other professional. Garrick belonged to an old Huguenot family, De la Garrique by name, who, like so many of their kindred in the seventeenth century, found a place of refuge on this side the Channel. His father, Lieutenant Peter Garrick, in the earlier years of last century was stationed at Lichfield with Colonel Tyrrel's regiment of dragoons. The lieutenant had married Arabella Clough, daughter of the vicar choral at Lichfield Cathedral, whose wife was an Irish lady — so that a mixture of French, English, and Irish blood flowed in the veins of the future Roscius. He was born at Hereford on the 19th of February 1716, his father, accompanied by Mrs. Garrick, being temporarily lodged there at that time with a party of dragoons. David's boyhood must have passed pleasantly enough among the genteel society at Lichfield, although his father was by no means rich; and while Mrs. Garrick may have managed to make ends meet, she does not seem to have been able to tie them in a bow.

The contemptible position of the players at this time, when an actor was a "rogue and vagabond" by Act of Parliament, would scarcely have induced any one of respectable parentage to dream of donning the sock or buskin as a means of earning a living; so that when, at eleven years of age, the youthful David, fired by the advent of a strolling company at Lichfield, actually produced Farquhar's "Recruiting Officer" for the delectation of a small audience of friends, there is no reason to suppose he was doing more than obeying that dramatic instinct which is so common to humanity.

Certain it is, that had his father and mother imagined the event in question betrayed any desire on the part of their son to take to the stage, they would not have countenanced the boyish production. We are told that David drilled his little playmates excellently, that he himself played Sergeant Kite, and one of his sisters was the chambermaid. Johnson, who, although a number of years older than David, had already become an intimate of his, refused, for some reason or another, to honour the occasion by writing a prologue!

About this time an offer was made by David's uncle at Lisbon, a prosperous wine merchant there, to take the lad, who was his namesake, under his care and provide for his future. This Lieutenant Garrick and his gentle wife, who were experiencing the difficulties of providing for a fairly numerous family on limited means, gladly accepted, and David was packed off alone to Lisbon, a fact which speaks for the confidence of the parents in the natural abilities of the lad; for a journey to Lisbon in 1728 was not the pleasurable trip it is to-day, especially for a youngster of his age. But David did not stay long in Lisbon; he was soon back again at Lichfield.

Shortly afterward (July 31, 1731) his father accepted an offer to go to Gibraltar on full pay, and remained away for nearly five years, during which time David kept up a continual correspondence with him from Lichfield, a correspondence that is now among the most interesting and unique of published documents. The letters from the lad do not speak highly of the education he was receiving at Lichfield; but they are all stamped with an individuality quite remarkable in one of his age. During these years David had several opportunities to enter the army as an ensign; but his filial devotion, which is one of the most beautiful features of his life, always restrained him, as it, in later years, curbed his inclination to become an actor during the lifetime of his mother.

When his father, now Captain Garrick, returned to England in the early part of 1736, he set about planning for David's future, and with the assistance of Mr. Walmsley, the Bishop's Registrar at Lichfield, who had taken a great personal interest in the lad, it was arranged he should go to the Rev. Mr. Colson, of Rochester, and be educated with a view to the bar. To London he went, accompanied by Johnson, who was proceeding thither with the manuscript of "Irene" in his pocket to start his literary battle; but David does not appear to have been supplied with the wherewithal to place himself under the tutorship of Mr. Colson; so he did not go to Rochester, but remained in London, and it was with some difficulty he raised money to enter as a student of the "Honourable Company of Lincoln's Inn." All plans were knocked on the head, however, by the death of Captain Garrick about a month after David had left his old home. Soon after this, the Lisbon uncle also died, and with his death David came into a welcome legacy, which now enabled him to taste the fruits of Mr. Colson's knowledge. By this time the magnetism of the stage was making itself felt, but he banished the idea of becoming an actor so long as his mother was alive.

Early in 1738 he was back again at Lichfield, having profited somewhat by his term at Mr. Colson's; but the nature of his course of learning there is not by any means clear. Meantime, his brother Peter, having abandoned the navy, the two arranged to set up as wine merchants, the sober-minded Peter conducting the Lichfield office and the sprightly David the London branch. Once settled in London, David, with his dramatic tastes, soon became an inveterate playgoer, and instead of paying the strictest attention to business, it is said he delighted to give mimicries of the theatrical performers at the clubs and coffee-houses where his wine was drunk! Becoming acquainted with Macklin, then among the performers at Drury Lane as Mechlin (his real name was M'Laughlin), Garrick developed a friendship with the queer Irishman, both being drawn together by the conviction that the regeneration of the stage lay in getting back to nature and away from the artificiality of the period, and, although Macklin latterly became his bitterest enemy, for five or six years they were inseparable.

Johnson, struggling on as a Grub Street hack, was now on terms of intimacy with Mr. Cave of St. John's Gate, the famous publisher of the *Gentleman's Magazine*, to which Johnson had become a contributor. For some reason, which does not exactly appear, Johnson mentioned Garrick's histrionic gifts to Cave, and the latter arranged in his room over the archway a rehearsal of Fielding's "Mock Doctor," with Garrick in the leading comic character, and several printers reading the other parts! The idea seems farcical to the reader to-day, and it is difficult to imagine what good Garrick expected to accrue from the performance, although we are told it "gave great amusement, and satisfied the sober Cave." But it shows that Garrick in his enthusiasm lost no opportunity of exercising his talent, and he even composed for the occasion a prologue, which was afterwards published in the *Gentleman's*.

We now arrive at Garrick's first appearance on the professional stage. As already stated, the gay young wine merchant had become a regular frequenter of the playhouses, and in those days there was much greater latitude in the laws regulating admission behind the scenes than there is to-day, so that the average "gentleman of fashion" had no difficulty in becoming acquainted with the players and managers if he were so inclined. It so happened, then, that during the run of a pantomime, entitled "The Harlequin Student," at the Goodman's Fields Theatre, in March 1741, Yates, the comedian, who played the leading part, became indisposed, and Garrick arranged with the manager to secretly appear as the harlequin. It was thus that his first appearance on the stage took place. Giffard, the manager, who was a man of much discrimination, recognised the latent histrionic ability of the young wine merchant, and would have given him a part in a regular play, but advised him to try his strength on a provincial audience before seeking the verdict of the town.

At this time Giffard was sending a troupe to Ipswich for a short season, and Garrick was offered a part. This he accepted, with that good sense which was one of his distinguishing qualities, and appeared under the name of Lydall, choosing that name, it is thought, to further hide his identity by suggesting relationship with the manager, whose wife was a Miss Lydall. He was warmly received by the Ipswich audience as Aboan, the black lieutenant, in "Oronooko;" and next played, with even greater success, Chamont in "The Orphan." But it was in the rollicking part of Sir Harry Wildair that he made his principal "hit" at Ipswich, although that part was afterwards regarded as one of his failures; as Captain Brazen, in the "Recruiting Officer," he was also very successful. Thus encouraged, it was but natural that he should determine to face a London audience as soon as possible, and on the 19th October of the same year (1741) his first great chance came, when he appeared at Goodman's Fields in the title rôle of "Richard III.," being described on the programme as "A gentleman who had never appeared before on any stage"—a fiction permitted in "the profession."

But at this point it is necessary to interpolate a few remarks on the condition of the stage, and the state of the dramatic art, at the time when Garrick made his first real start. Actors were almost social pariahs, and the performance of stage plays was prohibited, unless in Westminster, or where the sovereign in person was residing, and there a licence was necessary. Dramatic enterprise was practically paralysed. The Act of 1737, which was really an amendment of the Rogue and Vagabond Act, imposed all kinds of restrictions, and hedged the drama about with numerous difficulties. The Censor of plays is a remnant of this bigoted piece of legislation. But the Act was evaded, like many another before and since, and theatrical managers advertised a *concert* at so much, the play being given *gratis;* just as the old Scotch toll-keeper used to sell you on Sunday a small piece of cake for sixpence and give you a glass of whisky for nothing, and as entertainment managers to-day hold "free" Sunday concerts, to which you are admitted after augmenting the "silver collection." An art which laboured under such indignities could scarcely be supposed to flourish; so that it is no wonder the acting of the period was about as poor as the position of the player was contemptible. People were allowed behind the scenes in scores; they frequently invaded the stage while the play was toward; and on "benefit" nights the boards were crowded with seated auditors, and every entrance and exit blocked with chattering admirers of the *bénéficiaire.* It is said of a popular actor of the time that on one occasion, having forced his way through the crowd at the side when entering as Hamlet, and letting his hat fall as though lifted off by his hair rising in terror at the ghost—according to "tradition"—one of his admirers, a woman in a red cloak, who was seated on the stage, got up and replaced it! Then, imagine the beautiful Mrs. Cibber lying prostrate on the tomb of the Capulets—an old couch covered with a black cloth—amid a ring of onlookers; and fancy actors "escaping" into stage boxes crowded with fops and "women of fashion;" while in all the expensive parts of the house the audience kept up a constant chatter, the pitites sucked oranges, and children played unrestrained! Such things made stage illusion absolutely impossible; but there was really no attempt at this time to stage a play with any approach to propriety; declamation took the place of acting—

"From bard to bard the frigid caution crept,
Till declamation roared while passion slept;"

"art and actuality" were utterly neglected, stage royal ladies were usually attended, even in their most intimate and domestic scenes, by pages who never let down their sumptuous trains. A curious old satire, written soon after Garrick burst into fame, touches upon the characteristics of the acting of the period—

"Mark one who tragical struts up and down,
And *rolls* the words as Sisyphus his stone.
His lab'ring arms, unequal to the weight,
Heave, like a porter's when at Billingsgate.
But who is he that, mincing, trips along,
Making Lee's fury a mere op'ra song?
Two chattering daws next in some scene break loose,
And make a perfect rookery of the house.

. . . .

One heavily drags on a robe of state,
Lost in the diadem he seems to wear,
He mouths away and the spectators stare.
While this makes even the *freest* speeches grave,
That makes 'em dance like corks upon the wave."

Such is an imperfect glimpse at the deplorable condition of the stage, and the worse condition of the art, when Garrick essayed the part of Richard III. on

19th October 1741. We can dimly realise what an effect his natural style of acting must have produced on those who had become used to the ludicrous artificiality of the period. He chose Richard, after debating with Macklin which part he should first appear in, because that rôle was best suited to his figure—precisely the same reason that induced Kean to select Shylock for his first appearance at Drury Lane seventy-three years later. His performance was an immense success; there was no chanting of his words, no sing-song, no "dead level of declamation," and it was noted as a surprising novelty that he actually "seemed to identify himself with the part." The new acting, of course, gave rise to a storm of criticism from the old players. Quin said, "If this young fellow is right, then we have all been wrong," and there is not the slightest doubt that they had. But the victory lay with Garrick and his effort to restore nature to the stage.

A curious old newspaper criticism gives us at once an idea of his excellences, and, negatively, of the absurdities which obtained at the time. It remarks his nice proportions, his clear and penetrating voice, perfectly sweet and harmonious, without monotony, drawling, or affectation, "neither whining, bellowing, or grumbling, but perfectly free in its transitions, natural in its cadence, and beautiful in its elocution. He is not less happy in his mien and gait, in which he is neither strutting or mincing, neither stiff or slouching. When three or four are on the stage with him, he is attentive to whatever is spoke, and never drops his character when he has finished a speech, by either looking contemptuously on an inferior person, unnecessary spitting (!), or suffering his eyes to wander through the whole circle of spectators. His action is never superfluous, awkward, or too frequently repeated, but graceful, decent, and becoming."

Garrick continued acting anonymously with immense success, and had great difficulty in deciding whether he was better in tragedy or in comedy, coming near perilling his reputation by playing such puerile parts as Jack Smatter in "Pamela," and Clody in "Fop's Fortune"; but meantime he was studying Othello and Bayes ("The Rehearsal"), for both of which his manager, Giffard, had great hopes. On the second of December he took his benefit, and the veil was lifted, his name being published to the town. In Bayes Garrick made a great "hit," his wonderful powers of mimicry being displayed to the greatest advantage in "taking off" the mannerisms of his contemporaries, a performance which delighted the playgoers immensely. But although it was not to his manager's interest, he dropped this portion of the character at the request of those who were mimicked, as they represented that in holding them up to ridicule he endangered their livelihood. "The Champion" newspaper defended him, however, saying that his mimicking of the players was first done at Goodman's Fields to "excite curiosity and serve the proprietor," adding that Theophilus Cibber and "young Green" of Drury Lane were greatly applauded for the same thing, and that "I think it his least excellence. . . . For the best and only model is nature, of which Mr. Garrick is as fine a copy as he is of the players he imitates." A neat compliment. His Othello was as conspicuous a failure as his Bayes was a success. He was by nature unsuited for the part, and to make his natural defects worse, he played it in a bright scarlet coat with his face blacked like a negro's!

Garrick was always willing to accept advice, and never resented well-intentioned criticism, a trait that was no less marked in his later than in his earlier years. He took Macklin and Dr. Barrowby into consultation when preparing for his first performance of "King Lear," and arranged with them that they should be present when he essayed the part on 11th March 1742, and criticise it. This they did; they were not satisfied with Garrick's interpretation, although the audience received it well. They stated their objections, and the young actor noted them down, saying he would not play the part again until he had restudied it; but it had been announced for the following week, and he had to depart from this resolution. Macklin said that his second performance was not nearly so good as his first. Garrick, however, would not allow his two friends to see his next rehearsal, as he said their objections only constrained him in his playing. But when he next appeared in the part he seems to have made a great improvement, and, though only a young man of twenty-five, he had evidently thoroughly grasped the character of the aged monarch; for Macklin, when he had become Garrick's bitterest enemy, said, "In short, sir, the little dog made a *chef-d'œuvre* of it." Macklin was right, "the little dog" did make it his masterpiece, and it was said of him by a most discriminating critic in later years, that his Lear made him the greatest tragic actor, and his Abel Drugger ("The Alchymist") the greatest comedian.

The great feature of Garrick's Lear was his wonderful delivery of the "curse." This was so terrible that the audience is said to have seemed to shrink away and cower from it as if from a lightning flash, and the preparations—his throwing away his crutch, clasping his hands, and turning his eyes to heaven—inspired a strange forecast of terror. Foote, in his pamphlet on "The Suspicious Husband," gives the following minute description of the manner in which the great actor delivered the curse: "You fall precipitately on your knees, extend your arms, clench your hands, set your teeth, and with a savage distraction in your look, trembling in all your limbs, and your eyes pointed to heaven (the whole expressing a fulness of rage and revenge), you begin—

'Hear, Nature, dear goddess,'

with a broken, eager, inward utterance, and from thence rising in every line in loudness and rapidity of voice, till you come to—

'And feel
How, sharper than serpent's tooth,' &c.

Then you are struck, at once, with your daughter's ingratitude; and bursting into tears, with a most sorrowful tone of voice you say—

'Go—go, my people.'"

How simple all this seems! Yet how few are they who have ever been able to act the curse in accordance with Foote's analysis, and produce the terribly realistic effect which Garrick obtained. His wonderful simulation of madness produced by grief in the aged monarch is said to have been suggested to him by observing the awful despair of an old man who had dropped his child from a window. Some of his biographers say that Garrick witnessed the incident in a street near Goodman's Fields, but Grimm, to whom Garrick told the story, says it occurred in Ireland.

Reference has just been made to Garrick's good-natured deference to criticism, in which it is to be feared he was somewhat exceptional; but he sometimes carried this habit of listening to what was said about him to a point which produced morbid uneasiness, and made him alter his judgment with the passing hour. It is well, however, to look on the better side of this quality. Many years after he had become the most famous actor of his age, he wrote to the young author of a pamphlet in which he was somewhat kindly criticised: "I must assure you that I have more pleasure than uneasiness when I read a true, well-intended criticism, though against myself; for I always flatter myself that I can attain the mark which my friends may point to me, and I really think myself neither too old nor too wise to learn."

As a further instance of the consideration which he always gave to intelligent criticism, and an illustration of the scrupulous care with which Garrick studied and restudied all his parts, it may be stated that when he first played Macbeth, he spoke "Avaunt, and quit my sight!" as if Macbeth was still utterly oppressed and overcome by the sense of his guilt; but on an anonymous critic reasoning with him on the character of Macbeth, and arguing that the Thane was no coward, Garrick did not hesitate to modify his conception of the character. And, curiously enough, twenty years later another anonymous critic wrote objecting to the amended conception, and arguing that Macbeth should show signs of terror. Garrick then recollected his old critic who had first induced him to reconsider his study of the character, and said in reply to his new critic: "My notion, as well as execution, of the lines are, I fear, opposite to your opinion. Should Macbeth sink into pusillanimity, I imagine that it would hurt the character, and be contrary to the intentions of Shakespeare. The first appearance of the spirit overpowers him more than the second; but even before it vanishes at first Macbeth gains strength—

'If thou canst nod, speak too,'

must be spoke with horror but with a recovering mind; and in the next speech with him, he cannot pronounce

'Avaunt, and quit my sight!'

without a stronger exertion of his powers. I certainly, as you say, recollect a degree of resolution, *but I never advance an inch;* for, notwithstanding my agitation, my feet are immovable."

Like all great artists Garrick had his imperfections, and one of these was a doubtful ear for emphasis, which is rather surprising in one who was the apostle of nature on the stage. But there seems to be no doubt that he was sometimes mistaken in the meaning which he gave to his words by accentuation, and he actually followed the custom of other actors of the time by delivering that magnificent passage, after Macbeth has committed the murder of Duncan, thus—

> "Will all great Neptune's ocean wash this blood
> Clean from my hand? No—this my hand will rather
> The multitudinous seas incarnadine,
> Making the green one red."

The last line is absolute nonsense as it stands; but Garrick's good sense and sound judgment soon discovered the true reading—

> "Making the green—ONE RED,"

and so he afterwards delivered it. Mr. Fitzgerald mentions that Garrick was fond of suspensions, which the coarse ear of the audience, not attuned to delicate modulations of voice, would at times take for full stops. Thus, in "Hamlet," they insisted he made a full stop in one line—

> "I think it was to see—my mother's wedding."

So, too, in "Macbeth," at the line—

> "Plead like angels—trumpet-tongued."

The critics, says Mr. Fitzgerald, objected that by this pause the epithet "trumpet-tongued" was transferred to the "virtues" that came before. But Garrick could defend himself: "I really think the force of these four exquisite lines and a half," he wrote, "would be shortly lost for the want of an aspiration at *angels*. The epithet may agree with either, but I think it more elegant to give to the virtues, and the sense is the same." It was objected to him also that he put a pause improperly in the lines—

> "My thought, whose murder yet is but fantastical,
> Shakes so my single—state of man."

"If I do so," said Garrick, "it is a glaring fault; for the sense is imperfect. But my idea is this: Macbeth is absorbed in thought, and struck with the horror of the murder, though but in idea; and it naturally gives him a slow, tremulous undertone of voice. And though it might appear that I stopped at every word in the line more than usual, my intention was but to paint the horror of Macbeth's mind, and keep the voice suspended a little." As his biographer justly remarks, this is reasonable and original, and shows a nicety in Garrick's conception.

When in 1747 he entered into partnership with Lacy in the management of Drury Lane, of which he remained the guiding spirit for nearly thirty years, he set himself to institute many much-needed reforms, and these were hinted at in the famous prologue written by Dr. Johnson for the opening night, September 15th, of the new *régime*. The first thing that Garrick was to insist upon was, that all actors should play their parts according to the text, and not insult the audience by frequent appeals to the prompter, nor the poet by copious "gagging." He also set himself to rid the stage of the fashionable loungers who at that time had an almost unrestricted *entrée* behind the scenes, where they freely mingled with the performers, and often invaded the stage itself. But, above all, Garrick addressed himself to the task of restoring Shakespeare to the stage, and clearing away the fustian that had been grafted upon such works of the immortal bard as "The Tempest" and "Macbeth," by such daubers as Davenant, who had transformed the great tragedy into a kind of melodrama, it having been acted as such for about eighty years before Garrick restored it to its proper place.

It is surprising, yet it is only in keeping with a peculiar instability in the character of Garrick, that while he restored several of the bard's best works to the stage, freed from the impurities of would-be "improvers," he himself actually tampered with the work of Shakespeare in a manner little less reprehensible than that of those whose offence he had sought to remove. Thus, he did not hesitate to put an entirely new catastrophe to "Romeo and Juliet," and in 1772 he produced the most wondrous "Hamlet" ever staged. This version of Shakespeare's great tragedy was the joint work of Dr. Hoadley, Hopkins (Garrick's stage-manager), Steevens, and Garrick; they had all hacked and hewed at Shakespeare's work in a way that must have made the bard of Avon turn in his grave. The play became one of perpetual motion, and the grave-diggers were abolished, as being too rude for the Hoadley-Hopkins-Steevens-Garrick "Hamlet." This fearful and wonderful thing actually held the stage for eight years. But despite such errors of judgment as these, Garrick was a profound admirer of Shakespeare and a sympathetic interpreter of his characters, though he failed admittedly in Antony, Romeo, Othello, and Hotspur.

Garrick's management of Drury Lane was undoubtedly

the most brilliant period in the history of the famous playhouse, and at the root of all his great success lay hard work. He was unwearied in "drilling" his actors, and when we remember that he had not only to imbue them with some idea of natural acting, but had to break them away as much as possible from the conventionalities to which they had become accustomed, we may gain some idea of his task. He took infinite pains with all members of his company, whatever their rank, and rehearsed new plays for months. He himself would sometimes spend many weeks studying a part before he could satisfy himself that he had caught the character, and sometimes, even after long study, he would abandon a part in which he was doubtful of success.

The triumph of Garrick was the triumph of art over artificiality. He conceived art to be the imitation of nature, and the nearer the actor came to the presentment of nature in his stage picture the greater an artist was he. Churchill, in his famous "Rosciad," which appeared in March 1761, directed his satire with stinging effect at Quin and other artificial players of the period—

> "Parrots themselves speak properly by rote,
> And in six months my dog shall howl by note;"

but Garrick satisfied his sense of natural acting—

> "When reason yields to passion's wild alarms,
> And the whole state of man is up in arms,
> What but a critic could condemn the play'r,
> For pausing here, when cool sense pauses there?
> Whilst working from the heart, the fire I trace,
> And mark it strongly flaming to the face;
> Whilst in each sound I hear the very man,
> I can't catch words and pity those who can.
> . . . .
> Hence to thy praises, Garrick, I agree,
> And pleased with Nature, must be pleased with thee."

Johnson, who in later years did not continue the close friendship that existed between him and Garrick in their youth, was always a fairly accurate critic of the great actor. "Who can repeat Hamlet's soliloquy, 'To be, or not to be,' as Garrick does it?" said Boswell. "Anybody may," said Johnson. "Jemmy there," a child, "will do it as well in a week. Garrick was no declaimer; yet he was the only actor I ever saw whom I could call a master both in tragedy and comedy; though I believed him best in comedy. A true conception of character, and natural expression of it were his distinguishing excellences." Johnson preferred him in comedy, but there is no reason to doubt that Garrick was as great in tragedy. Some idea of his wonderful performance of Lear is gained from the fact that while playing in this character on one occasion he unconsciously pulled back his white wig revealing his own hair beneath, a thing which would have been fatal to any other actor; but the wonderful expression of his eyes and face held the audience spell-bound.

In this partial portrait of David Garrick no attempt has been made to touch upon his interesting relationship with his fellow-actors and authors; his personal character, which was as noble as his artistic gifts were transcendent, has also been left untouched, and only those features of his career that are likely to be of interest to the young histrion have been selected. Another remains to be noted.

An actor named Powell, whom Garrick had engaged just before he left for his continental tour, appeared at Drury Lane while Garrick was in Paris, and scored an instant success, filling the old playhouse as Garrick himself had filled it so often. The new actor took up character after character, and seemed to meet with complete approval in all. Garrick wrote to him from Paris a beautiful letter, full of generous enthusiasm at the success of one who threatened to be a serious rival to Roscius himself, and containing the gold of much good advice. The great player warned the new actor against taking up too many characters precipitately, but as he had already appeared in so many with so much success, now was the time for him to make sure of the ground he had gained. He warned him against clubs and flatterers. Should he ever sink into idleness, "those friends who have made you idle will be the first to forsake you. When the public has marked you for a favourite (and their favour must be purchased with sweat and labour), you may chose what company you please, and none but the best can be of service to you. . . . But above all, never let your Shakespeare be out of your hands or your pocket; keep him about you as a charm; the more you read him, the more you will like him, and the better you will act him. One thing more, and then I will finish my preaching. Guard against splitting the ears of the groundlings, who are capable of nothing but dumb show and noise. Do not trust your taste and feeling to the applause of the multitude. A true genius will convert an audience to his manner, rather than be converted by them to what is false and unnatural." The value of this advice is inestimable.

Again, when Garrick heard that Powell had been appearing in one of the ranting parts which had held the stage up to the time of Garrick, he wrote: "I am very angry with Powell for playing that detestable part of Alexander; every genius must despise such fustian. If a man can act it well—I mean to please the people—he has something in him that a good actor should not have. . . . I hate your roarers. Damn the part. I fear it will hurt him."

Of Garrick's farewell performances Hannah More,

who came up from Bristol to see them, said, "I pity those who have not seen him. Posterity will never be able to form the slightest idea of his perfections. The more I see of him the more I admire. I have seen him within these three weeks take leave of Benedick, Sir John Brute, Kitely, Abel Drugger, Archer, and Leon. It seems to me as if I was assisting at the obsequies of the different poets. I feel almost as much pain as pleasure."

He closed his long and honourable career in Don Felix on the tenth of June 1776, and on the tenth of January 1779 the grave in Westminster Abbey closed over the remains of an actor who, appearing on the English stage at a time of dramatic decay, by his great histrionic gifts breathed new life into the art of acting, and will, by reason of his exemplary career, live while the English Drama endures, as the model of a great actor and a perfect gentleman.

II

EDMUND KEAN

"In all romance, in all literature, there is nothing more melancholy, nothing more utterly tragic, than the story of the career of Edmund Kean. So bitter and weary a struggle for a chance, so splendid and bewildering a success, so sad a waste of genius and fortune, so lamentable a fall, can hardly be found among all the records of the follies and sins and misfortunes of genius." These, although the words of a hasty newspaper article, still stand as the most eloquent commentary on the wonderful career of a wonderful man. Although the generation which knew Kean as an actor has passed away, and we can only form our judgment of him at second-hand, the consensus of critical opinion acknowledges him as the greatest dramatic genius of the century.

Born in a bare and miserable chamber in the neighbourhood of Gray's Inn, on the fourth day of the chill month of November 1787, the natural son of one Aaron Kean by Ann Carey, a worthless pedlar and "strolling player," his entrance upon the stage of life was by no means auspicious. Some three months after the terrestrial début of the unwelcome little stranger the vagrom woman who had given him birth abandoned him; and then succeeds a period which, like the birth of Chawles Jeames Yellowplush, is "wropt in mist'ry." One

November night in 1789, however, the little fellow was found by a worthy couple in a dark doorway in Soho, "cold, hungry, and desolate." How he came there was never known, but the good people who discovered him took the child to their humble home and tended him as if he had been their own son.

Ann Carey, having been relieved of the trouble incidental to the nursing of a child in its first, and worst, two years, was soon on the hunt for her "property." And so it came about that in a few months the worthy couple referred to had to surrender the infant Edmund to the tender mercies of his mother, whose main object in regaining possession of him was to put him on the stage among the children in ballets and pantomimes, and so realise some profit out of his existence. She succeeded in obtaining a position for him as "the Cupid recumbent at the feet of Sylvia and Cymon" in one of Noverre's ballets at the Opera House—more on account of Edmund's remarkable beauty than through any good graces of the mother. But his seraphic countenance does not seem to have prevented the manager of Old Drury from engaging him after he had ceased reclining as Cupid to sustain the part of an imp in his pantomime. This was towards the close of 1790, when Edmund was completing the third year of his remarkable life.

Another period of mystery succeeds. It is not known to what uses the worthless woman turned her child, though she, no doubt, found him of material advantage in her calling as a strolling player and an attractive assistant in her peddling. Certain it is that his life during these early years was one round of infant misery and neglect; for Nance Carey seems to have been utterly devoid of the slightest particle of motherly love for her child. It is no wonder, then, that Edmund, when he was barely eight years of age, ran away from his mother, and joined a ship at Portsmouth; but he had not been many days at sea when he discovered that the life of a ship's boy was about as bad, if not worse than that from which he had sought to escape. And here a remarkable evidence of his extraordinary mimetic powers falls to be chronicled. Anxious to return to England, he would have deserted his ship at the first port, but for the uncertainty of his being able to find ways and means for the voyage home; and so he was driven to strategy.

He contrived to make the captain believe that a cold, contracted on board, had produced total deafness, supporting this statement in every look and gesture, so that both captain and crew were completely deceived. Afraid that mere deafness might not be held to relieve him from the necessity of performing his obnoxious duties, he pretended that the cold had settled in his extremities, rendering him so lame that he could not leave his bed!

The second deception proved no less successful than the first; he was attended to in his berth, and showing no signs of improvement, was placed in the hospital on the arrival of the ship at Madeira. There for two whole months he simulated deafness and lameness so remarkably that the doctors, completely deceived, prescribed his return to England as a last resource. This was exactly what he had been playing for, and on the return voyage he maintained his part so well that, during a terrific storm, when the ship was threatening to go to pieces every moment, he lay undisturbed, pretending to be so deaf that he could not hear the raging of the elements. On arrival at Portsmouth, we are told, he thanked those who carried him ashore by dancing a hornpipe and then disappearing among the purlieus of the docks. Here is unmistakable evidence of genius. The clever old schemer who recently simulated various diseases in the Paris hospitals, and made a considerable sum of money by pretending to be cured at Lourdes, must take a back place in comparison with the eight-year-old Edmund.

Back in London, young Kean found a home with his uncle, Moses Kean, a queer old entertainer of those days, who seems to have been quite a character in his way, and here his first regular training for his after career was begun, Miss Tidswell, the actress, who had taken an interest in the unfortunate child from his birth, teaching him the mechanical part of his art. At this time the lad was continually disappearing from home, performing acrobatic tricks and giving recitations at fairs and in taverns, an experience that must have been invaluable, although it was a practice which caused his guardians no little trouble, as they were driven to the necessity of fixing a brass collar round his neck, instructing those who found him to bring him back to the address in Leicester Square engraved thereon. Miss Tidswell, it is said, got him to rehearse his parts before a portrait, inducing him to suppose for the time that it represented the other characters in the scene, and this has been given as a reason for "his freedom from statuesque inflexibility and formal enunciation." But in the case of a genius like Kean it is scarcely likely that this had much to do with his stage manner. The idea seems a good one, however, as, despite Garrick's dictum, a love speech addressed to the portrait of a pretty woman should be more passionate than if it were addressed to a marble mantelpiece. Miss Tidswell would, further, appear to have been a firm believer in the principle that the actor must "learn to feel," as we find that after the death of old Moses Kean, for whom Edmund seems to have developed a strong attachment, she, "with a view to having his apostrophe, 'Alas! poor Yorick,' rendered in its true spirit, first made him say, '*Alas! poor uncle*,' in order that a reference to the lamented decease of Moses Kean might impart to his utterance the requisite combination of pathos, tenderness, and regret." From D'Egville the young Kean received those lessons in dancing, so necessary in his "strolling days," and which must have done much to give him ease on the stage, for "they move easiest who have learnt to dance." Angelo initiated him into the mysteries of fencing, and he became one of the most expert fencers who had ever appeared on the stage; while his musical voice was trained and developed by Incledon. We are told, moreover, that he never lost an opportunity of going behind the scenes, and he was ever on the alert to pick up every hint that could be turned to practical use.

With such training his great natural abilities were bound to shine forth to the fullest advantage; for he was only fourteen years of age when it is recorded that, a few days after he had entered upon the study of Shylock, he remarked to Miss Tidswell, "The devil is not so black as he is painted," and "Shylock is not such a devil as black-looking Mr. Kemble would have us believe."

Then ensued his long and weary career as a strolling player—performing in the open air at country fairs, in booths, in halls, in theatres, and always dreaming of the day when he would force his way to the footlights of Old Drury. "If I succeed I shall go mad," he often said after another disappointment; but it is characteristic of the indomitable spirit of the man, whose motto, as he told the Drury Lane committee in after years, was *Aut Cæsar aut nullus*, and in accord with the artistic impulse which moved and sustained him even in his earliest and most trying years, that he refused the offer of an engagement from Stephen Kemble to appear in London in 1807, on the ground that his powers had not then arrived at maturity.

An idea of the diversified nature of his performances in his later strolling days may be gathered from the fact that at Waterford, on the occasion of his benefit performance there, three years prior to his famous appearance as Shylock at Drury Lane, he played the hero in Hannah More's tragedy of "Percy," and "after the tragedy Kean gave a specimen of tight-rope dancing, and another of sparring with a professional pugilist. He then played the leading part in a musical interlude, and finished with Chimpanzee the Monkey in the melodramatic pantomime of 'La Perouse,' and in this character he showed agility scarcely since surpassed by Mazurier or Gouffe, and touches of deep tragedy in the monkey's death-scene, which made the audience shed tears." Herein we see the conscientious artist, who never scamped his work, no matter how unimportant that may have been, and never permitted the pressure of adverse circumstances to interfere with his devotion to his art. He is the true artist who would perform the part of a servant as carefully as he would impersonate the master.

In 1814, on the 26th of January to be precise, his great chance came; for it was on that date that he made his first appearance before a Drury Lane audience in the part of Shylock, choosing that rôle not because it was his best, but because in the gaberdine of Shylock his insignificant figure would not be so exposed as it would have been in the dress of Richard III., Othello, or Overreach, and so less liable to stand between him and the realisation of the character to a new and hyper-critical audience, whom he had not yet conquered. A chapter might be written about the 26th of January 1814; about the remarkable novelty of Kean's performance, the manner in which he traversed the most cherished stage traditions associated with the character of Shylock, and how he shocked his fellow-players by donning a black wig instead of the usual red one in which it had been customary to impersonate "the Jew that Shakespeare drew;" but all who have even a nodding acquaintance with the stage history of the century should know these things already. At this point, however, I would introduce the following passage from F. W. Hawkins's "Life of Kean":—

"From the earliest development of the drama in this country acting would appear to have divided itself into two distinct classes or schools—the romantic and the classic. The former relates to that style of acting distinguished by simple truth, fidelity to nature, and passion unfettered by the artificial restraints of the stage; the latter refers to the stilted, the declamatory, and the magniloquent. The first holds the mirror up to nature; the second does exactly the contrary. That acting in the Elizabethan period was of the turgid, pretentious, and premeditated description, there can be little doubt. In Thomas Betterton, who from 1662 to 1710 maintained against all competitors his position as the greatest actor of his time, the classic and romantic schools, with the more repellent prominences of the former tastefully softened down, met with a not inharmonious union. A discriminating student of nature, Betterton nevertheless sacrificed many beauties of truthful expression to negative objects of mere exterior grace. His successor, Barton Booth, who terminated a highly successful career of twenty-three years on the London stage in 1733, adopted the classical element in Betterton's acting to the exclusion of the natural; and James Quin, who made his first appearance at Drury Lane in 1715, followed in the same wake. In 1741 the classic school, with Quin's faultless elocution to sustain its popularity, stood high in vogue; but a regenerator was at hand. David

Garrick appeared at the theatre in Goodman's Fields on the 19th of October in that year, took the town literally by storm by the power of his genius and fidelity to nature, reduced the most cherished conventionalisms of the stage to disrepute, effected a very undignified collapse of the classic school, and sprang on to the ruins of the fallen temple with nature's banner in his hand. But Garrick did not live for ever. He died in 1779, and on the 30th of September 1783, John Philip Kemble appeared to undo all the good that his energetic little predecessor had accomplished by re-establishing art on the stage. Kemble's acting was utterly soulless. Possessed of a noble figure, he aimed exclusively at statuesque effects; and to the pursuit of this he sacrificed nature, passion, and the manifold beauties of truth. 'He was the statue of perfect tragedy,' writes Hazlitt, 'not the living soul.' His acting was studied, not unlaboured; his utterance was formal and measured, not easy, familiar, and natural. . . . Mrs. Siddons also belonged to the classical school, but there was more truth at times in her acting than in that of her brother. . . . In 1800 the supremacy of the classic school, then in the zenith of its popularity, was challenged by the rough, unstudied, and vigorously natural George Frederick Cooke, who excelled in the humorous, the caustic, and the mentally active, but who failed in characters requiring anything in the way of refined beauty, pathos, or tenderness, such as Hamlet, Othello, or King Lear. . . . He did not, however, succeed in diminishing the repute of the classic school; and Kemble moved on the acknowledged head of his profession until 1814. For a quarter of a century antecedent to that period the classic school had reigned supreme; but the Shylock, the Richard, and the Hamlet of Edmund Kean swept it, with its 'paw and pause,' from the stage, even as Garrick had done seventy-three years before."

For what is known of Kean's methods of study we have mainly to depend on second-hand information, although, in one or two instances, we have his opinions direct. But it is well known that during his early years, and while at the zenith of his fame, his industry was indefatigable; he would "sometimes remain up all night before the pier glass, endeavouring to realise by modulation, gesture, and action the conception at which he had arrived," and until he first jeopardised his reputation by failing to appear at Drury Lane in the "Duke of Milan," having overstayed with boon companions, he had never missed a single rehearsal, and had always been ready to take up his part at the appointed time.

Hawkins says of Kean that he was a fine physiognomist, studying the human face wherever he met it, and the tempers and passions of those around him. By these means he discovered new beauties in his author, new ideas combined in his head, new chords struck in his heart; and he expressed them all accordingly, because, while he studied the feelings of mankind, he studied the glass in which they were reflected and displayed. Like a painter and a philosopher, he let nothing escape him. He obtained conception and execution by the same means by which Michael Angelo became a great painter—by one continual exercise of his mind and his eye.

In illustration of this statement, continues his biographer, two instances of the manner in which Kean's performance was regulated by his observation of nature may be cited. On one occasion he and a brother actor named Giles had unintentionally trespassed upon some forbidden ground, when they were confronted by the enraged owner, who, on learning that they were players, wrathfully threatened to have the "vagabonds" put in the stocks. Giles resented the opprobrious epithet, challenged the farmer to a fight, charged his companion not to interfere, and Kean, sorely against his inclination, was compelled to remain a passive spectator of the encounter. The muscular prowess of the farmer soon decided the contest in his favour, but Giles, though physically overpowered, remained unsubdued in spirit, and in a paroxysm of defeated wrath, which convulsed his whole frame and seemed all but to suffocate him, he dragged open his shirt-collar, and tore it to ribbons. This incident was not lost upon Kean, who subsequently reproduced it in the last scene of "A New Way to Pay Old Debts," when he appeared as Overreach in London; and no one who saw him in that character could ever forget the appalling sensation produced by his manner, as, with face livid, eyes distended, lips swollen and parted at the corners, teeth set, and visage quivering, he dragged open his shirt-collar and tore it to ribbons. His falling on his back in the last scene of "Othello" was suggested by a similar incident in nature. He was giving a young officer some instruction in fencing, when he accidentally received an alarming wound in the breast, from the effect of which, becoming insensible, he fell to the ground on his back. When he recovered his senses, he immediately asked, "How did I fall?"

Speaking to Mrs. Garrick of the opinions passed upon his acting by the critics, Kean is reported to have said, "Those people don't know their business; they give me credit where I don't deserve it, and pass over passages where I have bestowed the utmost care and attention. Because my style is easy and natural they think I don't study, and talk about 'the sudden impulse of genius.' There is no such thing as impulsive acting; all is premeditated and studied beforehand. A man may act better or worse on a particular night, from particular circumstances; but although the execution may be less brilliant, the conception is the same. I have done all the things at country theatres, and perhaps better, before I was recognised as a great London actor; but the applause I received never reached as far as London." It is said, however, that Kean frequently proved the contrary of this, and that sometimes his wife, before whom he always rehearsed, had no idea of the real interpretation he was to place upon a part. When asked his reason for this, he replied, "I felt that what I did was right. Before, I was only rehearsing."

The great tragedian's firm friend, Dr. Francis of New York, tells us that "wherever he was, he was all eye, all ear. Everything around him, or wherever he moved, fell within his cognisance." It was this constant study of the idiosyncracies of his fellow-men that enabled Kean to make his characters "duplicates of nature," as one of his contemporary critics has put it. And Dr. Francis relates an anecdote with regard to Kean's Lear which is worthy of a place here. The tragedian said to the Doctor, who admired him most in Lear: "The real insanity and decrepitude of that old monarch of four score and upward is a most arduous part. I often visited St. Luke's and Bethlehem Hospitals in order to comprehend the manifestation of real insanity ere I appeared in Lear." Kean also expressed a wish to visit a New York asylum, to "learn if there was any difference in the insanity of John Bull and you Americans." Together with Dr. Francis and another this wish was carried out, and Kean's visit to a New York asylum was marked by evidences of that incipient insanity which he himself had inherited from the Careys through his mother. He entered the asylum gate with a double somersault, spoke deliriously when going through the place, and purposed making an end of his life by jumping from the ridge of the roof, to which the party had ascended in order to view the panorama of the surrounding country. He was all right in the evening when the Doctor asked him how he studied phases of disordered intellect, and the tragedian replied, "By the eye, as I control my lion." (He had a lion for a pet.)

Even in the gloaming of his life, when he was no longer the man of bright intellect and giant mind who had conquered the dramatic world in 1814, this propensity for studying the people around him remained as strong as ever. During his declining days at Richmond, where he died on the 15th of May 1833, he used to frequent the Castle Hotel, and it was in a room there one night that he was asked by a friend when he studied. Indicating a man on the other side of the room, who was very much intoxicated, and who was labouring to keep up the appearance of sobriety, Kean replied, "I am studying now; I wish some of my Cassios were here. They would see that instead of rolling about in the ridiculous manner they do, the great secret of delineating intoxication is the endeavour to stand straight when it is impossible to do so." It was in those days, too, that he had occasion to give evidence before a Parliamentary Committee on Theatres, and strongly advocated large theatres, saying, "I think the intellect becomes confined by the size of the theatre. The larger the stage the better the actor, and the less observable are his faults, which is a material consideration."

George Henry Lewes has written of Kean with rare insight: "He was an artist, and in all art, effects are regulated. The original suggestion may be, and generally is, sudden and unprepared—'inspired,' as we say; but the alert intellect recognises its truth, seizes on it, regulates it. Without nice calculation no proportion could be preserved; we should have a work of fitful impulse, not a work of enduring art. Kean vigilantly and patiently rehearsed every detail, trying the tones until his ear was satisfied, practising looks and gestures until his artistic sense was satisfied; and having once regulated these, he never changed them. The consequence was that, when he was sufficiently sober to stand and speak, he could act his part with the precision of a singer who has thoroughly learned his air. One who often acted with him informed me that when Kean was rehearsing on a new stage, he accurately counted the number of steps he had to take before reaching a certain spot, or before uttering a certain word; these steps were justly regarded by him as part of the mechanism which could no more be neglected than the accompaniment to an air could be neglected by a singer. Hence it was that he was always the same; not always in the same health, not always in the same vigour, but always master of the part, and expressing it through the same symbols."

I have confined this chapter to Kean, the great tragedian; the actor who, despite an insignificant figure, a voice "harsh and discordant in its upper register," worthily earned the opinion of the critic who wrote in "Chambers's Encyclopædia," "Kean was amongst actors what Byron is amongst poets, Napoleon amongst generals." But while his brilliant, if meteoric, career is full of encouragement for the young player, who may be plodding at his art in the chill obscurity of "rural shades," it also presents the reverse side of the medallion, with an awful warning inscribed thereon.

III

WILLIAM CHARLES MACREADY

Born on 3rd March 1793, William Charles Macready was the son of a London actor of no particular eminence, but one whose painstaking was a habit that descended to his son. When at the close of the 1796–97 season William M'Cready left Covent Garden Theatre, after ten years' connection with that house, his reputation was summed up in the couplet—

"Though than M'Cready there are many better,
Who, pray, like him, so perfect to a letter?"

Obviously, Macready's father was a useful, but not a brilliant, member of the Covent Garden company during these ten seasons. During the residence of his parents in London young Macready was sent to a preparatory school in Kensington; but he could not have been more than six years of age when the scene of his life changed to Birmingham, whither the elder Macready had gone the year after his secession from Covent Garden, to settle down as a manager of the Midland Circuit, having, three years previously, been engaged in management at Birmingham during the provincial season. It was to a school in St. Paul's Square, Birmingham, presided over by "an irascible old pedagogue named Edgell," that

William Charles was sent, and here he would appear to have distinguished himself mainly in recitation. He learned by heart long extracts from Shakespeare, Milton, Pope, and Young, and these, writing in his "Reminiscences," he says, "have been of some service to me in accustoming my ear to the enjoyment of the melody of rhythm."

His mother, a worthy woman of no great histrionic attainments, who played "utility" in her husband's productions, had great difficulty in those early days in teaching William Charles the proper value of letters in the spoken word, the line "'Appy, 'appy, 'appy pair" being for a time a perfect *pons asinorum* to the young pupil. But this attention bestowed by his mother on the cultivation of a sense of rhythm was of great value in later years, when, despite Fanny Kemble's adverse criticism, all who heard him agree in saying that his sense of rhythm was especially marked. Fanny Kemble says that "His want of musical ear made his delivery of Shakespeare's blank verse defective, and painful to persons better endowed in that respect. It may have been his consciousness of his imperfect declamation of blank verse that induced him to adopt what his admirers called the natural style of speaking it; which was simply chopping it up into prose." One would hesitate to suggest prejudice on the part of this fair critic, but Macready was certainly not conscious of any such defect, and, as Mr. Archer suggests, it may have been his practice of putting sense first and form second—thereby reversing the Kemble procedure—that led Miss Kemble to form this judgment.

In Lady Pollock's little book, on "Macready as I Knew Him," she gives Macready's criticism of a new reading suggested for the celebrated passage, line 3, book ii., of "Paradise Lost"—

> "Or where the gorgeous East, with richest hand,
> Showers on her kings, barbaric pearl and gold,"

in which the pause was changed as follows—

> "Showers on her kings barbaric, pearl and gold."

Macready, Lady Pollock tells us, pointed out that in the first place the kings here designated were not barbaric; and in the next place that such a pause destroyed the music and rhythm of the line, ending it meanly with "pearl and gold." This surely displays a keen sense of rhythm, and it is important to note the connection between his mother's early teaching and the actor's subsequent attainment.

Young Macready was sent to Rugby School at the midsummer session of 1803, and here his taste for theatricals was amply gratified. He began by playing small female characters in the productions of the scholars, and rose eventually to such parts as Zanga in "The Revenge." But it was as a reciter that he shone among his fellow-students, having only one rival, the Robinson who was afterwards Master of the Temple, in elocution. The future tragedian had then no desire to go on the stage; indeed, he never, to his last hour, took any great degree of pride in his profession, and he approved of his father's intention of sending him to the bar. But there is evidence that he was not entirely opposed to the enjoyment of the actor's triumphs in his note on his last recitation at Rugby, when he speaks of the "inward elation I felt in marking, as I rose slowly up, the deep and instant hush that went through the whole assembly." The beginning of his stage career was not, however, of his seeking; and Macready stands almost alone in this respect. Most actors go on the stage out of a consuming love for the actor's art; not so Macready. He was drawn to the stage against his own will and by the force of adverse circumstances.

The elder Macready, having succeeded in his management at Birmingham, must needs launch out on a more ambitious undertaking at Manchester, with the consequence that at the end of his first season in Cottonopolis (1808), he found himself in such difficulties that he could not pay his son's school bills for the second half of that year. When William Charles went home at Christmas he learned the state of things for the first time, and, renouncing all thought of the bar, boldly embarked, at the age of sixteen, less two months, as his father's lieutenant in all the risk and worry of provincial theatrical management. Six months of financial misery in Manchester, and then he undertook the supervision of the Newcastle Theatre for a short summer season, proceeding to London in the autumn to learn fencing under Angelo, and to study the leading actors of the day.

Returning to Manchester, he was present when his father surrendered himself to a sheriff's officer to be lodged in Lancaster Castle, and on the following day the youth assumed the management of his father's company at Chester, finding himself face to face, single-handed, with all the soul-saddening trials incidental to the management of a strolling company on an impoverished treasury. So hard-pressed was he that he had to leave his own watch in pawn at Chester, and those of three of his company at a posting station on the road, in order to reach Newcastle in time to open the theatre on Boxing Day, 1809. The season there was fairly successful, and before its close the elder Macready was out of jail and at his post once more, but the trial of such an experience to a lad of scarcely seventeen, who had left school less than a year before, must have been most severe, and was not calculated to improve a fiery, irascible temper, inherited from his father.

Macready's father seems to have got on his feet pretty soon again, for the summer of the succeeding year (1810) found him once more manager in Birmingham, where, on the 7th of June, William Charles made his first appearance in his father's production of "Romeo and Juliet"—"the part of Romeo by a Young Gentleman, being his first appearance on any Stage." The performance was very satisfactory to all parties concerned. It was repeated on the 11th, and on June 13th the "young gentleman" appeared in "Monk" Lewis's "Adelgitha" as Lothair, a performance which he repeated three days later in the name of "Mr. William M'Cready." Young Norval and Zanga were his next assumptions, and on July 30th his performance of the homicidal hero in "George Barnwell," which he regarded as the best of his early efforts, was the last of his initial season in Birmingham. Thus, the young actor had stepped at once into "the lead," skipping those long years of strolling misery which left their mark on Edmund Kean; and for four years he held the leading place in his father's companies, working hard, but always on leading characters, and not on thankless parts which brought no credit. Two successful seasons at Bath followed, some other provincial engagements, and so to London. What an ideal progression! Not one player in a thousand has found the road to success so easy—and yet Macready was not happy!

Although Kean was only six years older than Macready, and his great performance of Sir Giles Overreach had taken place in January 1816, and he was undoubtedly a formidable rival to the new claimant for popular favour, "the brandy-bottle," as Mr. Archer says, "was already doing its work; and though Kean's great name was a power in the land even to the day of his death, seventeen years later, his genius was a mere wreck before Macready's had reached maturity." Macready well knew that his gifts were not like Kean's—his was not the power to capture the public at one stroke, as it were, and to hold it captive. He had to work steadily and arduously for its approval, and, as his biographer remarks, "he had not unreasonably long to wait for a share of popularity, which gradually increased until he stood without a rival at the head of his profession." As usual on the occasion of a new actor in a leading rôle tempting fate in London, there was a council of war as to the part in which Macready should open at Covent Garden. There was a tacit understanding, of course, to avoid contrast with Kean in any of the parts identified with that great tragedian, but a somewhat timid policy fixed upon Orestes in "The Distressed Mother" for the venture. The chief merit of this part seems to have lain in the fact that it had not been revived for several years, and so Macready, who had acted it with considerable success in the provinces, had not to overcome the recent impression left by any great predecessor. His first appearance in London, on 16th September 1816, was entirely successful; for though the critics were unanimous in condemning the choice of play, they agreed that the new actor showed great power and true passion.

Thus, warmly welcomed by the critics and approved by the public, Macready's rise was sure and steady. His first real "hit" was his creation of Rob Roy in Pocock's wretched adaptation of Scott's novel, produced at Covent Garden on 12th March 1818, and with his performance of Richard III. on 25th October 1819, he had thoroughly established himself in public favour as a tragedian of the first rank, the success of his Richard saving Harris, the manager of Covent Garden, from ruin at a critical time in the history of that theatre. His Virginius, first undertaken on May 17th of the following year, set the seal to his claim to pre-eminence in the tragic drama, for Kean was daily losing his grip of the public. His two years (1837–38 and 1838–39) of management at Covent Garden were fruitful in dramatic enterprise, and did much to foster the higher drama at a time when it was inclined to languish, and the same may be said of his brilliant régime at Drury Lane (1841–42 and 1842–43). Then followed his first visit to America. He opened in New York on 25th September 1843, and toured the States as far south as New Orleans, westward to St. Louis, and northward into Canada, as far as Montreal, a tour of immense material and artistic success terminating at Boston on 14th October 1844. Macready netted a clear profit of £5500 from this transatlantic enterprise, and "Hamlet," he chronicles, brought him more money than any other play in America. Back in England, he was mainly seen in the provinces, with only occasional visits to London, till the middle of 1848, when he set out on his farewell tour in America. The story of that fateful visit, and the Forrest riots which it occasioned, is one of the most interesting and exciting in the annals of actors and their quarrels; but we have not time to dwell upon it here. It was in June 1849 that Macready returned, and he retired from the stage, after a series of brilliant farewell performances at Drury Lane, in February 1851. In the closing years of his life he experienced much domestic sorrow, passing away peacefully on Sunday, 27th April 1873.

As an actor, how does Macready compare with the other great figures of the English drama, with his predecessor in the headship of the contemporary stage?

The questions raised cannot be decided in the space at our command; indeed, they have been a fruitful source of discussion for many years. Macready was uniformly conscientious, always in earnest, ever striving how to improve his art, and when he performed for the last time, after his long and arduous career, he confessed that he was still a student of those Shakespearian characters which it had been his task to reproduce upon the stage so often. With Kean this conscientiousness was awanting, in his later years at least, although it can never have been very strongly present, else it should have rendered his eventual *débâcle*—moral, physical, and artistic—impossible. But there is no reason to doubt that Kean was gifted with a genius to which Macready could not lay claim. As Mr. Archer says, the very fact that questions arise as to Macready's art, show that his position is not assured.

Perhaps the best criticism of Macready is that set down by George Henry Lewes in these words: "In Edmund Kean and Rachel we recognise types of genius; in Macready I see only a man of talent, but of talent so marked and individual that it approaches very near to genius; and, indeed, in justification of those admirers who claim for him the higher title, I may say that Tieck, whose opinion on such a matter will be received with great respect, told me that Macready seemed to him a better actor than either Kean or John Kemble; and he only saw Macready in the early part of his long and arduous career." Judged by Lewes's own standard, that the greatest actor is he who is greatest in the highest reaches of his art, his estimate would be regarded as correct; for Macready was only greatest in parts like Werner, Richelieu, Iago, or Virginius, and, if we except his performance of King Lear, he always fell short when representing any great Shakespearian hero.

Writing of Macready again, Lewes says: "He did not belong to the stately declamatory school of Kemble, but in all parts strove to introduce as much familiarity of detail as was consistent with ideal presentation. His 'touches of nature' were sometimes a little out of keeping with the general elevation of the performance, and he was fond of making a 'point' by an abrupt transition from the declamatory to the conversational; but whenever he had an emotion to depict, he depicted it sympathetically and not artificially; by which I mean that he felt himself to be the person, and having identified himself with the character, sought by means of the symbols of his art to express what that character felt; he did not stand outside of the character and try to express its emotions by the symbols which had been employed for other characters by other actors. There is a story told of him which may be exaggerated, or indeed may not be true of him, but which at any rate illustrates so well the point under notice, that it may be repeated here. In the great scene of the third act of the 'Merchant of Venice,' Shylock has to come on in a state of intense rage and grief at the flight of his daughter. Now, it is obviously a great trial for the actor to 'strike twelve at once.' He is one moment calm in the green-room, and the next he has to appear on the stage with his whole nature in an uproar. Unless he has a very mobile temperament, quick as flame, he cannot begin this scene at the proper state of white heat. Accordingly, we see actors in general come bawling and gesticulating, but leaving us unmoved because they are not moved themselves. Macready, it is said, used to spend some minutes behind the scenes, lashing himself into an imaginative rage by cursing *sotto voce*, and shaking violently a ladder fixed against the wall. To bystanders the effect must have been ludicrous; but to the audience the actor presented himself as one really agitated. He had worked himself up to the proper pitch of excitement which would enable him to express the rage of Shylock. I have heard Madame Vestris tell a similar story of Liston, whom she overheard cursing and spluttering to himself, as he stood at the side scene waiting to go on in a scene of comic rage."

Macready's assiduous study, his constant endeavour to improve his art, are well illustrated in a story told by James Murdoch. Murdoch says that an American senator, on a visit to London, being disturbed in the small hours of the night by hearing some one, as he thought, shout "Murder!" repeatedly in all sorts of tones, rushed into the passage and shouted "Hallo, there! hallo!" when his landlady put her night-capped head out of the door, and begged him not to be alarmed, as it was only Mr. Macready the tragedian. The next morning an apologetic note brought an explanation. Macready had that night been playing Macbeth, and being dissatisfied with his treatment of the murder scene, had been "submitting the words 'murder' and 'murdered' to a kind of aspirated and husky utterance in different degrees."

Although the incident just described related to the tragedian's early years at Drury Lane, the same care and painstaking characterised him to the end, and he liked to think that his last performance of a part was his best. Thus, writing to his friend Wightwick in 1840, he says: "I think it cannot be wrong to endeavour to preserve in my acting an equal, or to supply a greater, quantity of passion, with less of exaggerated attitude and overstrained expression—*i.e.* distortion of countenance—a more sustained deportment with less quantity of voice—and to avoid the melodramatic practices you speak of, which in Kean (*the* Kean) himself were blots upon the bright genius of a superlatively great actor, and which were never—*never*—to be detected in Mrs. Siddons, in Talma, in Kemble, or in Miss O'Neill."

We are brought into intimate touch with Macready the man and the artist in Lady Pollock's chatty little book already quoted. As illustrative of his genuine artistic temperament, Lady Pollock mentions that Macready, when a very young man, once in a dream saw and heard definitely and distinctly a friend lately dead, who came to address to him words of admonition. He woke in extraordinary emotion, and the image of this man filled his mind for long afterwards. Whenever he was to act Hamlet, he summoned up the passion of that dream.

And we get a valuable insight into Macready's ideas of teaching in the account Lady Pollock gives of a lesson in reading which she had of him one day. She had selected a piece well known to her. "Now," said Macready, "if you wish really to learn, you must accept something, on the contrary, that will bring out your faults in strong relief. I don't want to accuse you of vanity, but this looks like it." Her ladyship confesses to being troubled by his "penetrating look," but she agreed to accept a piece with which she was not familiar, and Macready chose a difficult part of Milton, because "he would exhibit her worst faults." She read the part of the Attendant Spirit ("Comus") from "Before the starry threshold" down to "the palace of Eternity," and Macready's criticism ran as follows: "Here," he said, "is a spirit addressing mortals, and telling them of the exalted places where he has his dwelling, and whence he has descended to communicate with them: not in the tone which you might well use to tell me you were hemming that pocket-handkerchief (pointing to one she had left unfinished on the table), could such a communication be made; yet you have read in just such a tone, and you failed not only in impressiveness, but in distinctness. Your words merged into each other, and your mouth was not sufficiently open. You lost your breath, too, in the passage of 'calm and serene air.' In reading, you must carefully consider how long your breath will serve before you enter upon a period. A breath taken in the wrong place destroys the power of expression."

On a further attempt by her ladyship, the tragedian said: "That is much better read; but there were many of the same faults; your mouth not well opened, and not a sufficient variety of tone. Sweetness alone is not enough—a constant sweetness tires the ear; you must do yourself a violence, and shock yourself by the sound of your own voice in its full power, before you can so command its inflections as to make a good reader. Practise alone for a time, aiming only at distinctness; then consider the breathing, and then think of the expression."

At the epoch of his final retirement from the stage Macready had entertained thoughts of adding to his income by teaching elocution, but he abandoned the scheme "with the conviction that no man could teach feeling, and to teach the rest without that, would only be to graft his own manner on another." He was of opinion that every actor necessarily had a manner of his own, every individual had a manner, and in an imitator that manner would become a mannerism; he "did not wish to be the founder of a mannered school."

The tragedian also said that he had only seen one amateur who, if transported to the stage at once, would have made a great public performer. This was a Miss Wellesley, who, in charm and even in diction, was not inferior to the celebrated Mrs. Jordan. She had a spontaneous grace, which in the professional actress was the result of elaborate care. He had seen Mrs. Jordan insist upon the repetition of a scene twenty times in order to make sure of the effect of her exit. This amount of labour, he said, was not to be found in amateurs, nor if it were, would that alone succeed, not even when allied, as in many cases it was, to remarkable intelligence and sensibility. What was wanting in the amateur was freedom—freedom of passion, freedom of diction, freedom of movement. The whole training of drawing-room life, where self-restraint was the one great lesson, went against it.

Macready's "Reminiscences, Diaries, and Letters," edited by Sir Frederick Pollock, bring the reader into immediate touch with the thoughts of the great actor. As human documents these self-revelations are among the most interesting in the whole range of our personal literature, and they contain much of value to the student of acting, for whose benefit we will briefly examine them. Writing of his boyhood in Birmingham, and when he was a student at Rugby, Macready says: "My great amusement in my summer holidays at Birmingham was in seeing plays, and in acting some of my own compositions with my brother and sister." Thus early do we see the dramatic instinct manifesting itself.

Referring to his early days on the stage at Birmingham, he writes: "I worked in earnest on the part submitted to me for each performance, endeavouring to improve on its repetition. It was only on Sundays that the theatre, being locked up, was free from the presence of all employed in it. I used to get the key, and, after morning service, lock myself in, and pace the stage in every direction to give myself ease, and become familiar in my deportment with exits and entrances, and with every variety of gesture and attitude. My characters were all acted over and over, and speeches recited till, tired out, I was glad to breathe the fresh air again. *This was for several years a custom with me.*"

He also mentions in another place that he had made a practice, whenever he was at the seaside, of reciting aloud in the solitude of the shore, with the object of strengthening his voice, and giving him complete confidence of utterance.

On the mistake of striving after "points" Macready, in a note comparing Edmund Kean's Richard with Cooke's, remarks: "His (Kean's) personation was throughout consistent, and he was only inferior to Cooke where he attempted points upon the same ground as his distinguished predecessor. These points have often proved stumbling-blocks to actors and false lights to the discernment of audiences. The instances have not been rare in the drama's history when frequenters of theatres on the occasion of an actor's or actress's first essay in any popular character, have reserved their judgments for the effect to be produced by one line or one speech, the particular point rendered famous by some preceding player; and the artist has as often been betrayed into laboured efforts to give prominence to such isolated passages, instead of relying on his penetration into the full depths of the poet's intention and the perfect comprehension of his one large and grand idea."

He speaks strongly on the necessity of the actor always doing his best, no matter what the size or the nature of the audience may be. "It was a rule with me," he writes, "to make what profit I could out of a bad house, and before the most meagre audience ever assembled it has been my invariable practice to strive my best, using the opportunity as a lesson; and I am conscious of having derived great benefit from the rule. I used to call it 'acting to myself'; as, indeed, it was, transferring the study of a character from my own apartment to the stage, where it was much less irksome; for in the solitude of a lodging to continue over and over again the repetition of passages with strict attention to one's elocution, deportment, gesture, and countenance, guarding against exaggeration, whilst lashing oneself up to the highest strain of passion, and this without any stimulus, or any test beyond the individual's trust of having struck the chord aright, was a sort of darkling procedure, groping or feeling one's way, that called upon me often for strong efforts of perseverance, being more trying to the constancy and patience of the student than falls to the lot of any other art: for in others the advances made are visible in the comparison of the works completed; but the player, by dint of repeated effort, must perfect himself in tones, attitudes, looks, of which he can only learn the effect under the nervous excitement of experimenting their power on the uncertain sympathies of a heterogeneous assembly."

Touching the old question of "acting at rehearsals," Macready, writing in 1817, says: "It was the custom of London actors, especially the leading ones, to do little more at rehearsals than read or repeat the words of their parts, marking on them their entrances and exits, as settled by the stage-manager, and their respective places on the stage. To make any display of passion or energy would be to expose one's self to the ridicule or sneers of the green-room, and few could be more morbidly sensitive to this than myself. But the difficulty of attaining before an audience perfect self-possession, which only practice can give, made me resolve to rehearse with the same earnestness as I would act; reasoning with myself that if practice was of the value attributed to it, this would be a mode of multiplying its opportunities, of proving the effect of my performance, and of putting myself so much at ease in all I might intend to do, that the customary nervousness of a first night would fail to disturb or prevent the full development of my conceptions. Upon making the experiment I may quote Dryden's line ''Tis easy said, but oh! how hardly tried!' I found it much more difficult to force myself to act in the morning with the cold responses and the composed looks of Miss O'Neill, Young, and the rest, than at night before the most crowded auditory. Frequently in after years, when I have given certain directions to actors rehearsing, the answer has been, 'Sir, I never can act at rehearsal, but I will do it at night,' to which I had only one reply, 'Sir, if you cannot do it in the morning, you cannot do it at night; you must then do something because you must go on, but what you cannot do now, or cannot learn to do, you will not be more able to do then.' The task I found a very hard one, but I fought successfully against my *mauvaise honte*, and went doggedly at it. By this means I acquired more ease in passing through the varieties of passion, confirming myself in the habit of acting to the scene alone, and, as it were, ignoring the presence of an audience, and thus came to wield at will what force of pathos I was master of."

Writing of a visit to Glasgow in 1819, he speaks of visiting a lunatic asylum for the purposes of his art; and he remarks, "as the aim and object of all true art is the skilful blending of the real and the ideal, it becomes the student's study to store his mind abundantly with facts, at the same time that he gives free scope to the exercise of his imagination." From the Glasgow asylum he took thence "lessons, painful ones indeed, that in after years added to the truth of [his] representations."

Finally, Macready's conception of the actor's art is

that so strikingly expressed in those beautiful lines of the poet Campbell, which he quotes with approval—

> "For ill can poetry express
>   Full many a tone of thought sublime;
> And painting, mute and motionless,
>   Steals but a glance of time.
> But by the mighty actor brought,
>   Illusion's perfect triumphs come;
> Verse ceases to be airy thought,
>   And sculpture to be dumb."

PART III

LIVING ACTORS ON THEIR ART

I

SIR HENRY IRVING

No living actor has written so much or spoken so often on the Art of Acting as Sir Henry Irving. The famous tragedian has not been content with perfecting himself in his art, so that his great natural genius might be brought to bear with the fullest effect on the numerous impersonations with which he has enriched the Anglo-Saxon stage; he has from time to time taken us into his confidence, as it were, and revealed to us his inner mind on the art of which he is such a brilliant exponent.

In some respects, Sir Henry Irving's stage career says all that might be said with regard to his conception of the actor's art; for the man who has, in a great measure, to be thanked for the dignified position to which the stage has attained in the later part of the present century can only entertain the very highest opinion of his calling. But we are not so much concerned at present either with the dignity of the stage, or the actor's status as an artist, as with the practice of the histrionic art, and since even the most discriminating critic can only formulate his judgment from the observation of outward effects, it is necessary, when our desire is to learn something of the means whereby these effects are produced, to go for our information to those who practise the art. As I have remarked at the outset, Sir Henry has given us on many occasions the benefit of his thoughts on the essentials of good acting and the best methods of preparation for a stage career. And it will not be gainsaid that no one is more entitled to speak with authority on all that pertains to stagecraft than this famous tragedian, who, by sheer weight of genius, hard work, and self-devotion to his art, has long been acknowledged the foremost English actor of his day—even by those who, like Mr. W. Archer, have passed through a period of doubt and unbelief to respectful admiration. Nor has any great actor ever brought to the consideration of the subject a mind more unprejudiced, a judgment more equable, an enthusiasm more real.

Of Sir Henry Irving's acting we are not, of course, able to enter into any analysis within the scope of this work; but it may be mentioned that during his first American tour one bright transatlantic critic wrote of him, "Take away Mr. Irving's personality, and he is merely an awkward player." This is an easy method of criticism, as one of his biographers remarks: "Take away his imagination, his insight, his artistic conscientiousness, his facial expression, and his vast experience, and you have nothing left but mannerisms, which you may denounce at large." The justice of this is too obvious to call for exposition; for a man's personality is the "immortal part" of him, and it is mainly in their personality that great actors outshine their fellows. If there were no such thing as personal distinction, then, surely, would the stage, and life itself, be void of interest.

But it was also an American critic who, in a line, passed upon Irving's acting the most pregnant, as it is the most truthful, of all the volume of criticism which that has elicited. The writer in question said that Irving's acting was "impersonation as distinguished from mere representation." This, as we shall presently find, is precisely what Sir Henry himself has always aimed at accomplishing; this is what he considers to be the basis of all good acting.

In an address, which he delivered to the students of Harvard University on 30th March 1885, Sir Henry, then Mr. Irving, entered into a most exhaustive exposition of the Art of Acting, and were it within our present province to vindicate the place of acting among the arts, there was much that Sir Henry said to the Harvard students, eleven years ago, which might be quoted to-day in proof of the fact that acting in its highest sense—"the art to which Roscius, Betterton, and Garrick owed their fame"—is one of the highest callings to which gifted men and women can devote their lives. As becomes one whose greatest triumphs have been the impersonation of Shakespearian characters, we find that Sir Henry regards the study of Shakespeare as one of the first things to which the young actor or the stage aspirant should devote his attention. And this is most natural, since in the works of the immortal dramatist we find the whole gamut of human passions touched, as that has never been touched before or since, by the hand of the master. "When I was a boy," says Sir Henry, "I had a habit which I think would be useful to all young students. Before going to see a play of Shakespeare's I used to form—in a very juvenile way—a theory as to the working out of the whole drama, so as to correct my conceptions by those of the actors; and though I was, as a rule, absurdly wrong, there can be no doubt that any method of independent study is of enormous importance, not only to youngsters, but also to students of larger growth." Herein we discern the early determination to do everything that he took in hand with that thoroughness and independence which have been the distinguishing features of Sir Henry Irving's inspiring career, and the main factors—after his genius—in his remarkable success. The advice is eminently worthy the attention of all serious students.

A firm believer in the "Life School," and one who has scant sympathy with Diderot's theory, Sir Henry is careful to appraise at its true artistic value everything that may assist the actor in perfecting the mechanical part of his art. "There can be no objection to the kind of training that imparts a knowledge of manners and customs, and the teaching which pertains to simple deportment on the stage is necessary and most useful; but you cannot possibly be taught any tradition of character, for that has no permanence. Nothing is more fleeting than any traditional method of impersonation. You may learn where a particular personage used to stand on the stage, or down which trap the ghost of Hamlet's father vanished; but the soul of interpretation is lost, and it is this soul which the actor has to recreate for himself. It is not mere attitude or tone that has to be suited; you must be moved by the impulse of 'being'; you must impersonate, and not recite."

But he hastens to say that the study of elocution is a most important point in the Art of Acting. "And in elocution," says Sir Henry, "one great difficulty is the use of sufficient force to be generally heard without being unnaturally loud, and without acquiring a stilted delivery. The advice of the old actors was that you should always pitch your voice so as to be heard by the back row of the gallery—no easy task to accomplish without offending the ears of the front row of the orchestra. And I should tell you that this exaggeration applies to everything on the stage. To appear to be natural, you must in reality be much broader than nature. To act on the stage as one really would in a room, would be ineffective and colourless. I never knew an actor who brought the art of elocution to greater perfection than the late Charles Mathews, whose utterance on the stage appeared so natural that one was surprised to find when near that he was really speaking in a very loud key." There is a great danger, however, in a young actor spoiling the impersonation of any character he may be endeavouring to portray by paying too much attention to elocution, by forgetting that faultless intonation and perfect pronunciation are only means to an end, not the end itself. "I will give you a year," said Sir Henry Irving to a young man who had gained some applause by a rattling delivery—"I will give you a year to learn that speech so that you will make your audience imagine for the moment that you have not got it by heart." We find the tragedian's theory on this very important point stated with great clearness in his preface to an English translation of Talma's "Réflexions sur Lekain et l'Art Théâtral," in which he says: "Let the student remember, first, that every sentence expresses a new thought, and therefore frequently demands a change of intonation; secondly, that the thought precedes the word. Of course there are passages in which the thought and language are borne along by the stream of emotion and completely intermingled. But more often it will be found that the most natural, the most seemingly accidental, effects are obtained when the working of the mind is visible before the tongue gives it words." Any one who has had the privilege of seeing Sir Henry Irving in Hamlet or Iago will fully appreciate the value of this advice, his delivery of the difficult soliloquies which occur in these parts being matchless, and their "seemingly accidental effects" being produced on the principle here laid down.

The backbone of good elocution is pronunciation, and in this connection Sir Henry thinks there is something to be said which, in ordinary teaching, is not sufficiently considered. "Pronunciation on the stage," he says, "should be simple and unaffected, but not always fashioned rigidly according to a dictionary standard. No less an authority than Cicero points out that pronunciation must vary widely according to the emotions to be expressed; that it may be broken or cut, with a varying or direct sound, and that it serves for the actor the purpose of colour to the painter, from which to draw his variations. Take the simplest illustration, the formal pronunciation of 'A–h' is 'Ah,' of 'O–h' is 'Oh'; but you cannot stereotype the expression of emotion like this. These exclamations are words of one syllable, but the speaker who is sounding the gamut of human feeling will not be restricted in his pronunciation by the dictionary rule. It is said of Edmund Kean that he never spoke such ejaculations, but always sighed or groaned them. Fancy an actor saying thus, 'My Desdemona! Oh, ŏh, ŏh!' Words are intended to express feelings and ideas, not to bind them into rigid fetters. The accents of pleasure are different from the accents of pain, and if a feeling is more accurately expressed, as in nature, by variation of sound not provided for by the laws of pronunciation, then such imperfect laws must be disregarded and nature vindicated. The word should be the echo of the sense."

Passing on to that vital element of acting which concerns the physique of the actor, and which, in the opinion of some people, is the very thing that prevents their conceding to the player a position as an artist, Sir Henry Irving has some very sensible observations to make, and some eminently practical advice to offer. "It is necessary," says he, "that a good deal of attention should be given to bodily training. Everything that develops suppleness, elasticity, and grace—that most subtle charm—should be carefully cultivated, and in this regard your admirable gymnasium (at Harvard University) is worth volumes of advice. Sometimes there is a tendency to train the body at the expense of the mind, and the young actor with striking physical advantages must beware of regarding this fortunate endowment as his entire stock-in-trade. That way folly lies, and the result may be too dearly purchased by the fame of a photographer's window. It is clear that the physique of actors must vary; there can be no military standard of proportions on the stage. Some great actors have had to struggle against physical disabilities of a serious nature. Betterton had an unprepossessing face; so had Lekain. John Kemble was troubled with a weak asthmatic voice, and yet by his dignity, and the force of his personality, he was able to achieve the greatest effects. In some cases a superabundant physique has incapacitated actors from playing many parts. The combination in one frame of all the gifts of mind and all the advantages of person is very rare on the stage; but talent will conquer many natural defects when it is sustained by energy and perseverance."

One of the most noteworthy features of Sir Henry Irving's career as an actor and a manager has been the immense amount of historical research he has expended over every one of his productions, so that the whole play might be a faithful mirror of the time and events which have furnished the poet with his theme. Indeed, those petulant detractors who are always to be found disparaging the work of greater men, in their paucity of complaints against Irving, the tragedian, have sometimes charged Irving, the stage manager, with burying Shakespeare in a mass of historical detail; though, curiously enough, another class of would-be "smart" people have found in him "an excellent stage manager, and an indifferent actor." But Sir Henry has himself given the best reply to these snarling censors, who consider it a mark of learning to find fault, and all sensible people agree that the actor who fails to thoroughly acquaint himself with the manners and customs of the times in which the dramatist has placed the character he has undertaken to embody, neglects one of the most important duties imposed upon him by the art which he presumes to follow. On this point, Sir Henry, in an address delivered at the sessional opening of the Philosophical Institution, Edinburgh, on 9th November 1891, says: "Not only must his (the actor's) dress be suitable to the part which he assumes, but his bearing must not be in any way antagonistic to the spirit of the time in which the play is fixed. The free bearing of the sixteenth century is distinct from the artificial one of the seventeenth, the mannered one of the eighteenth, and the careless one of the nineteenth. And all this is quite exclusive of the minute qualities and individualities of the characters represented. The voice must be modulated to the vogue of the time. The habitual action of a rapier-bearing age is different from that of a mail-clad one—nay, the armour of a period ruled in real life the poise and bearing of the body; and all this must be reproduced on the stage, unless the intelligence of the audience, be they ever so little skilled in history, is to count as naught."

Another most important consideration is touched upon in the same address—the necessity for the individual actor to so comport himself while on the stage, from his first entrance to his final exit, that even when he has no words to speak he still continues to bear himself with a nice regard to the character of his part, and its relationship to the whole; to maintain, in short, the illusion which the spoken words justify and suggest. "Why," says Sir Henry, "the action of a player who knows how to convey to the audience that he is listening to another speaking, can not only help in the illusion of the general effect, but he himself can suggest a running commentary on what is spoken. In every moment in which he is on the stage, an actor accomplished in his craft can convey ideas to the mind."

A final extract from Sir Henry's Edinburgh address: "'In the consideration of the Art of Acting it must never be forgotten that its ultimate aim is beauty. Truth itself is only an element of beauty, and to merely reproduce things vile and squalid and mean is a debasement of art. There is apt to be such a tendency in an age of peace, and men should carefully watch its manifestations. A morose and hopeless dissatisfaction is not a part of true national life. This is hopeful and earnest, and, if need be, militant. It is a bad sign for any nation to yearn for, or even to tolerate, pessimism in its enjoyment; and how can pessimism be other than antagonistic to beauty? Life, with all its pains and sorrows, is a beautiful and a precious gift; and the actor's art is to reproduce this beautiful thing, giving due emphasis to those royal virtues and those stormy passions which sway the destinies of men. All, actors and audience alike, must bear in mind that the whole scheme of the higher drama is not to be regarded as a game in life which can be played with varying success. Its present intention may be to interest and amuse, but its deeper purpose is earnest, intense, sincere."

II

MR. J. L. TOOLE

THE life-history of Mr. John Lawrence Toole, the prince of humourists, the quaintest of comedians, the most universally popular figure on the English stage, is as well known to every intelligent person as, say, the story of the Spanish Armada, or that of the battle of Waterloo. Where is there one amongst us who is not aware that the popular comedian is the second son of the late Mr. James Toole, a well-known civic toast-master, and a respected employee of the Honourable East India Company; that he was educated at the City of London College; that at twenty he was entered as a clerk in a wine merchant's office; that in those early days he was an enthusiastic amateur actor; that in the year 1852 his first professional appearance was made at Ipswich; that for almost half a century he has been one of the most acceptable contributors to the "gaiety of nations"?

Not to know these things is to confess one's self woefully out of touch with modern history. For Mr. Toole, like his "dear friend Irving," has for many years been as much a part of our national life as Mr. Gladstone or Lord Salisbury. Indeed, it is an open question whether, if a plebiscite were taken, "the people" would not manifest a greater measure of personal liking for the great comedian than for the distinguished statesman. And this could easily be understood, as the one gets much closer to their hearts than the other.

It is a rare gift that enables an actor to prove as great a master of pathos as of humour; though psychologists tell us that the source of laughter and the source of tears lie side by side, and on that ground the great comedian should be equally effective in pathetic parts, while, inversely, the great tragedian should have a keen sense of humour. Be that as it may, it is rarely that we find an actor who displays a complete mastery over both these passions; but Mr. Toole is admittedly such a rarity. Those whom he has excited to laughter by the quaint humour of his Mr. Doublechick, his Paul Pry, or his Don, he has as readily moved to tears by the exquisite pathos of his Caleb Plummer.

Mr. Toole contributes the following bright little article:—

Some of my most valuable experience was gained in my early days in Edinburgh, when the stock-company was an institution in the land. One did not benefit merely from the change of bill, but from the fact that one was brought into contact with the great actors of the day, when they came to the provinces on their "starring" engagements. Such, at all events, was my experience in Modern Athens, for I have always considered that I profited greatly from playing with the stars that visited the Scottish capital. For instance, I played Touchstone to Miss Helen Faucit in "As You Like it," and as Cloten in "Cymbeline," and Glavis in "The Lady of Lyons," I also appeared with that most gifted actress. My performances were also very kindly noticed by the critics, and I might say that in the first week of my appearance I had become something like a favourite in Edinburgh. During my stay there I subsequently played in many parts with Phelps, when he came on a starring engagement, and also with Charles Mathews.

These were days of hard work. When a stock-actor I played as many as eighteen parts in one week, some of them new studies entirely! But although the work was hard, and rough, if you will—for one's best could not be expected when one had to study another part while playing a new one, or go home late at night to study for rehearsal next day—still the experience was well worth having, making things easier for one in later years. But nowadays there are no stock-companies for the young actor to join, and the chances of gaining good experience are very few, with the result that we have many young men actually obtaining positions on the stage in modern comedy simply because they know how to dress well and speak well—necessary things no doubt in an actor, but by no means the sum total of acting.

When the idea of going on the stage first took possession of me—and for many years after I had become an actor—I made it a habit to study all kinds of acting, carefully noting details and incidents of business, not for the purpose of mere imitation—which is the great fault of many young actors' performances to-day—but regarding them as lessons by which I might profit. Much has been said about "teaching" the art of acting, but I have always maintained that the best "school" for the actor is the theatre. Let the aspirant go to the theatre and there study the best acting of the day, in tragedy and comedy; let him observe how the actor obtains his effects, how he speaks a pathetic speech, how he delivers a comic passage, noting that while one actor does it one way another may do it with equal success in a different way.

Then let him try if he can produce similar effects by the same means, or by others which will suggest themselves to him from studying a good model; let him try his ability in private, among his friends, and he will soon learn whether he is boring or interesting them. If the experiment is favourably received, and he is prepared to risk all the uncertainties and hardships inseparable from a stage career, then let him join some company—a provincial repertoire company, for example—where he may be given small parts in different pieces, and let him study *behind* the footlights what he has been studying from the front. Above all, let him master his Shakespeare. These things done, he will get his chance some day, and I wish him luck!

J. L. Toole

III

MR. GEORGE ALEXANDER

"I WAS born at Reading, on 19th June 1858," said Mr. George Alexander to the ubiquitous interviewer recently, "my father being Scotch and my mother English. At the age of ten I was sent to Dr. Benham's school at Clifton, but on my father returning to Scotland in 1872, I commenced to attend the High School at Stirling. While I was still a scholar my initial appearance, as the saying goes, 'on any stage,' took place. This happened at beautiful Bridge of Allan, at the house of the late Mr. Davenport Adams. His son, since well known as a dramatic critic, was the author of a classical burlesque entitled 'Jupiter Æger.' I was offered, and accepted, a small part in its production by a band of amateurs at his father's house, and this experience, trifling though it was, served to kindle in me a burning desire for histrionic distinction. I was fifteen years of age at the time, and at seventeen I left Stirling, and was sent to Edinburgh to take up the study of medicine. Frankly, I didn't like it the least little bit in the world, and I said so. Without direct intervention of my own, however, my father altered his mind about my career, and after a couple of terms in the Scottish capital, I proceeded to London and entered the office of a silk mercer, a friend of my father's. Once in the

Metropolis, of course, I was enabled to indulge my bent for theatre-going to the full, so that I speedily developed into a first-nighter of the most pronounced and persistent type. How far the varied experience so gained may have moulded my own methods as an actor, I leave you to judge.

"The Thames Rowing Club, of which I became a member, is, as you know, 'great' on amateur theatricals. In their company, my Charles Courtley in 'London Assurance,' and my Jack Wyatt in 'The Two Roses,' were, I think, two of my best assumptions. But I will never forget what I owed, as Charles Courtley, to Mr. Henry Neville, while I would also fain record my indebtedness to the late John Clark and the late Horace Wigan. I had many laughable adventures as an amateur —notably once in 'Hamlet,' when the wigs failed to arrive, while the prompt-man added to the general confusion and terror by making the clock of Elsinore Castle strike fourteen!

"I was by this time fairly well known as an amateur, and in 1879 was asked to take part in 'The Critic,' as played at Cromwell House under the auspices of Lady Freak. Mr. F. C. Burnand and the late Mr. Samuel Brandram both took part in the performance, which was one of the greatest successes that have ever fallen to a band of amateurs. This was the turning point in my life. People were exceedingly kind to me, notably Mrs. Stephens, once so celebrated herself. Therefore, on a night in September 1879, I 'took the plunge,' by appearing at the Theatre Royal, Nottingham, in Mr. Sydney Grundy's 'The Snowball.'"

To take up the thread of the story where Mr. Alexander leaves off. A London engagement soon followed, his first appearance in the Metropolis being at the Lyceum in "The Two Roses," and his part Caleb Deecie. In 1882 he played Claud Glynne in "The Parvenu" at the Court Theatre; and later accompanied Miss Wallis on a provincial tour, playing Benedick, Orlando, and other leading parts. He then settled down in London, and for the next two or three seasons was seen at various theatres, appearing with Mr. and Mrs. Kendal at the St. James's, and with Miss Mary Anderson at the Lyceum. Engaged in 1884 for Sir Henry Irving's American tour, after the company returned he undertook, on 19th December 1885, to play Valentine in "Faust" at the Lyceum, and during the run of the piece later filled the title rôle. At the same theatre he also appeared as Ulric in "Werner," Silvio in "The Amber Heart," and Macduff in "Macbeth." This period of his professional career and his association with Sir Henry, Mr. Alexander remembers with the utmost delight, speaking of his old chief as his "master and friend." It was in March 1890 that Mr. Alexander enrolled himself among the actor-managers, opening the Avenue Theatre at that time with the highly-successful farcical comedy "Dr. Bill," in which he played the title part. In February of the succeeding year he took over the management of the St. James's Theatre, where he has produced many excellent and successful plays, the names of which, from "Sunlight and Shadow" to "The Prisoner of Zenda," are pleasantly familiar to all playgoers. Mr. Alexander's position in the front rank of actors has been won by conscientiousness and earnestness, wedded to distinguished histrionic gifts.

In the course of a recent address to a Leeds Dramatic Society, of which Mr. Alexander is the President and godfather, he made the following allusion to his own personal experience: "I am sufficiently young to be one of the actors who studied in the amateur school. For many years before I became a professional actor I devoted every hour I could steal from the commercial pursuits in which I was engaged—and which I studiously neglected—to the study of the stage; and blossoming into an amateur, I learned a great deal from the aid which the clubs to which I belonged obtained from professional 'coaches.' Speaking from my own experience, one of the first pieces of advice I would give to any amateur dramatic club is, that the best available professional coach should be called in as stage manager. From the old theatrical hand more can be learned in a couple of hours than will come in weeks spent in the difficult task of finding things out for one's self. In the course of time the pupil may outstrip his master, but he will ever be thankful for a good grounding in the rudiments of his education."

Mr. Alexander has kindly written the appended article at my request:—

It is impossible to deny that in our art of acting, as in all other arts of value, the one great, indispensable thing is work; work of the proper kind among the right folk. In old days the work on the stage was more varied, by reason of the old stock system, than is the case to-day. More varied, but not altogether more useful to the art it served, seeing that the deliberation and careful study, concentrating on one part alone, was impossible with the ancient haste which waited on the assumption of many within a week. What was gained in confidence was often lost in refinement.

To my mind the modern actor is best trained in one of two schools. First, the amateur school—so much despised, so greatly the stage's creditor; second, the country training of a sound repertoire company, where too many plays are not embarked upon, and yet the so necessary variety is not wanting. Of course, I am aware that many capable actors begin and end on the London stage, and play few parts, yet play them well. But I fancy they would be better actors for a better training. The advantages of a repertoire experience are so obvious I will not press them. The advantages of a good amateur training, the playing of good parts in good pieces and before many very different kinds of audiences, may be thought to want more demonstration. Let it suffice here for me to say, that I for one greatly applaud it.

I shall be told, no doubt, that there are stage tutors who can teach their pupils more than the mere rudiments of their art, and of this fact I am well aware; but although the pupil may take his lessons, he may have very few opportunities of putting the knowledge which he is understood to have received to the test of actual practice. I gladly admit that there is great value in such teaching, and that, providing the pupil has the aptitude for the work, it may go some way towards making him an actor; but *without the practice*, if an aspirant have an earnest love for the art he is cultivating, my impression is, that he would learn more as a super on the Lyceum stage, if he took note of, and profited by, the excellent examples of histrionic perfection always to be seen there.

As regards the method of study, what is there to say? So many men—so many methods. All one can advise the beginner is to judge for himself by means of practice, not by theory—*in*duction, not *de*duction! My own method is a slow and painful one to me, as I always set out with the purpose of getting thoroughly into the character I am to present before I trouble to acquire the words. It *may* come of a sudden, this insight into the man I would be; it generally *does* come after long wrestlings with lazy inclinations, and the distractions occasioned by the contemplation of the other parts in the play—all of which I see and know before my own.

But, as I have said before, each must work out his own salvation in this direction, and where one man may climb with ease, another will be certain to slip. One really cannot give a "lead" in study. It all resolves itself into the one pregnant word with which I began—"work." There is no hope for the laggard, or the careless. He may succeed as a buffoon by reason of some natural ridiculousness—an actor he will never be.

George Alexander.

IV

MR. H. BEERBOHM TREE

THIS eminent actor is another of the many who have found their way to the professional boards *viâ* the amateur stage. He is consequently a firm believer in the value of amateur theatricals as a means for recruiting the stage; but there are few who have found the pathway to dramatic fame so free from briars and thorns as the late manager of the Haymarket, and the owner of that more ambitious temple of Thespis which opens in the spring of 1897—Her Majesty's Theatre. This may account to some extent for his holding the belief that "if a man has it in him, he will feel a part when he reads it, and require nothing but a little practice in order to present his conception." Born in 1853, in London, where his father Julius Beerbohm, the second son of a wealthy German landowner, had settled down as a grain merchant some eleven years previously, the youthful Herbert was educated partly in England and partly in a school at Schnepfeuthal, and to avoid the conscription entered his father's London office in 1870.

Soon after this date he joined the Irrationals A.D.C., and assuming for the first time the stage name of Tree, he achieved local fame as a member of that amateur company. So encouraging was his progress here that he determined to make his pastime his profession, and appearing as Grimaldi at a Globe matinée, in aid of the Stafford House Fund, he met with a welcome that could have left no doubt in his mind as to his having chosen wisely. During the next five years, it has been said, he played at least a hundred parts in a hundred different plays without making any extraordinary impression on the world of playgoers, although his impersonation of Marquis de Pontsablé in the opera of "Madame Favart," and his Prince Maleotti in "Forget-me-Not," were universally praised. But Mr. Tree had become an actor of the first repute before he made his memorable "hit" as the Rev. Robert Spalding in "The Private Secretary." His impersonation of this character, which he is said to have based on a meek and mild young curate whom he had encountered at a Bloomsbury supper-table, was not merely the saving of an indifferent comedy, but the making of a phenomenal success.

Then came his performance of Macari in "Called Back," which has since become a stage tradition, and the awakening of dramatic London to the fact that in Mr. Tree the English stage possessed an actor of singular power and originality. His next notable performance was that of the German swindler in "Jim the Penman," and then in April of 1887 he entered the ranks of actor-managers as lessee of the Comedy Theatre, where he opened with the still popular "Red Lamp," in which he played the rôle of Paul Demetrius. In September of the same year he moved into the Haymarket, and there, up till the summer of 1896, he presided over the destinies of that historic house with great benefit to the dramatic art, and no small profit to his managerial pocket, the history of his reign at the Haymarket being writ large in the annals of the contemporary stage. Any notice of Mr. Tree's stage career would be incomplete without mention of his Hamlet. The melancholy Dane has been described as a character in which no actor could completely fail; but Mr. Tree has to be ranked with those great actors who have found in it new beauties and subtle truths that have escaped previous interpreters. It is the hope and belief of all enthusiastic playgoers that a long era of continued good fortune and artistic enterprise lies before this gifted actor at Her Majesty's.

Mr. Beerbohm Tree writes of his art with much literary charm :—

It has always seemed to me that acting is not the mere reproduction of a personality, and that the higher aim of the artist is to let his personality be subservient to the part he is playing. I know that many whose opinions are entitled to high respect are not of this mind; but I for one decline to admit the opposite contention, for, to carry on this argument to its logical conclusion, the literary artist should make all his characters act and talk as he himself would act and talk. It seems to me that the actor should possess so supple a nature that he should be able to play any part for which his physique does not render him unfit. To do this he must have the courage of his convictions, for in essaying any rôle with which he has not already familiarised the public, he will be opposed by the advocates of the vested rights of tradition — he will be warned that he must not enter the new domain, and he will have to fight his way step by step. I do not contend that the actor has so wide a field for the exercise of the purely imaginative in his work as has the literary artist, for instance, for the actor is always limited by being himself the medium through which to express his own emotions; but I do maintain that even if, for the time being, the artist misses something of that personal popularity which is more readily gained from an obtrusion of his individuality, he will gain by the exercise of his art, satisfy his own aspirations, and win the applause of those whose approbation he most values, those whose approbation should "o'erweigh a whole theatre of others."

Good acting is of more necessity than beauty of person, and will always be more appreciated by the bulk of playgoers. To present in a flash the heart of an incident is one of the most important qualifications of the actor. So far as I can judge, there is only one way to act, and that is by impersonation. But for some occult reason there are still those who regard the art of acting as a sort of co-operative store, with many departments. We used to have "the heavy man," the "leading man," the "light comedian," and the "utility man"; the "leading lady," and the "heavy lady." And it was once a serious matter if any one of these entrenched on the province of the other. There is now a tendency to merge these departments. There is another cant expression which I should be glad to see eliminated from the dictionary of acting—that is "character acting." All acting is character acting, or ought to be.

The very alpha and omega of dramatic art is illusion. Everything which tends to add illusion, to stimulate the imagination of the audience, is legitimate on the stage; everything that detracts illusion is illegitimate. That is the only rule. There may have been a tendency to over-elaboration, to over-decoration, which might swamp the beauty of the poet, but in that matter taste must always be the final arbiter. I cannot think that the public would nowadays be so readily inclined to listen to Shakespeare's works, did they not receive that splendour of setting which modern ingenuity and resource have placed at the disposal of the stage manager of to-day. Mechanical devices should be avoided if illusion can be got without them, but it should be remembered that the real thing is very often not nearly so effective as the make-believe.

Viewing the stage as a whole, I think that the present should be a prolific period for the drama, for never was there a time of more honourable rivalry to produce the best within their reach than is going on to-day among authors and actor-managers. If there is a widespread taste for the lighter forms of entertainment, there is, at the other extreme of the dramatic school, a great and vital demand for serious work. We have recently passed through a period of undue pessimism, and now the more realistic or morbid drama has, in its turn, given place to romance. And so it will ever be. Romance and realism have been perennially interchangeable; they do not interfere with each other.

H. Beerbohm Tree

V

MRS. KENDAL

MRS. KENDAL has been styled "The Matron of the Drama," and her rights in the title are too conspicuous to call for definition. While we may agree to differ from her in some of the opinions she is wont to enunciate off the stage, we must all respect her independence of thought, her purity of purpose, and we cannot but recognise her immense gifts as an artist. The circumstances of Mrs. Kendal's birth were sufficient, almost, to make her a notable woman—the twenty-second child of parents who came of a long line of histrions, the youngest member of a family whose oldest was T. W. Robertson, the dramatist, whom Mrs. Kendal "never knew . . . except as a man grown up—such a great many brothers and sisters came between us;" and, over and above these things, did she not first see the light on "the very day and hour" when her father, up till then a prosperous manager on the Lincolnshire theatrical circuit, learned that he had "lost everything" in "the railway mania or some other burst of speculation" which had "reached into Lincolnshire"? It is rather remarkable that the first and last of this truly formidable family should have been so singularly endowed; but as to the why and wherefore I do not purpose making any inquiry, nor shall I be tempted to speculate upon the inscrutable ways of an all-wise Providence, who made the child, born in the hour of financial disaster, some sixteen years afterwards, the happy means whereby her parents were relieved from the task of struggling for their livelihood. Suffice it that in Mrs. Kendal the Robertson family seems to have reached the height of its artistic development; for it is doubtful if from its abundant seed another such flower will spring.

In her early days "Our Madge"—as she was then called, the Matronship of the Drama being still a long way off—showed talents in so many directions that her parents were in some doubt as to her future, and were only certain that she was "going to be something." She played boy parts, and "burlesque boys," to boot, and she sang with so much promise that it was difficult to determine whether a career as an actress or as a singer lay before her. Some time later she still seems to have hovered between the two, for we find her singing "the first note" in the new Theatre Royal at Nottingham, where she acted for a time before proceeding to Hull as leading lady in another new Theatre Royal there, with William Brough as manager.

At Hull, too, she was as yet undecided as to her special line of acting, playing in everything from Lady Macbeth to Papillonnetta—"a lady with wings" —in one of Brough's burlesques, in which the young actress also "danced a *pas seul!*" But prior to her Nottingham engagement, Miss Robertson had made her initial appearance in London, where, at the Haymarket, she played for six weeks with Walter Montgomery, and during that time she acted Desdemona to the Othello of Ira Aldridge, an actor who had "the shadowed livery of the burnished sun" direct from nature, and who "always picked out the fairest woman he could to play Desdemona with him, not because she was capable of acting the part, but because she had a fair head." Shades of Shakespeare! Fancy sweet Desdemona's chief attribute being that of "the lassie wi' the gowden locks." We must assume, however, that Miss Robertson as Desdemona had something more than her qualities as a blonde to commend her impersonation of this exquisite creation of Shakespeare's genius.

From Hull, where she had played Lady Macbeth to the Thane of Samuel Phelps, Miss Robertson returned to the Haymarket, then under the management of Buckstone, and here she remained for seven years, meeting her husband, who was also a member of Buckstone's company, and marrying him on one of their occasional trips into the provinces. It is scarcely necessary to remark that no theatrical marriage has been more happy in domestic results, or more fruitful in artistic enterprise. But Mr. W. H. Kendal, like the husbands of most clever women, has never received all that recognition which his polished and artistic acting fully merits, having always been viewed in conjunction with his gifted wife. As becomes a gallant husband, however, he has found his fame in his wife's success.

After leaving the Haymarket, Mrs. Kendal went to the Court Theatre with Mr. Hare to play Lady Flora; then to the Prince of Wales's to play in "Peril" and "Diplomacy," and in 1879 Mr. Kendal and Mr. Hare became the joint managers of the St. James's Theatre, the dual management continuing with the happiest results till July 1888, since when Mr. and Mrs. Kendal have been "in town," or "on tour" in the provinces or beyond the sea, to the constant delight of all who can appreciate acting of the highest artistic merit.

Mrs. Kendal favours me with the following:—

I am often asked if I can specify the secrets of popularity in an actor; but who can define that mysterious "something" which brings him or her into immediate sympathy with an audience? If it were easy of definition, it might be easy of acquirement, but it is neither the one nor the other, and the only thing we can say is that the man or woman who does not possess this peculiar quality is never likely to exercise a great hold on the public, even though he or she may be, in every other respect, a very admirable artist. The dramatic instinct, and the subtle human sympathy which brings one into touch with the feelings of one's fellow-creatures, cannot be acquired either by study or by perseverance; and if these are among the inner secrets of success—as I have a shrewd suspicion they are—then it will be seen why there is no royal road to dramatic fame. Many actors, however, have attained a certain measure of popularity on account of the public being told they were great actors until it began to believe; but unless an actor has the necessary "staying power," unless he possesses this mysterious "something," no amount of critical laudation can ever serve to retain a popularity which may have been so earned, as the public is wonderfully correct in its judgments, and the public is the actor's first and final court of appeal.

As I have said, a man or woman may be a very good artist, and yet lack this indefinable quality which makes for success or greatness. It is a common thing to see very finished actors never rising beyond second or third rate parts, while others of far less artistic finish climb to the very front and draw the public to see them in every new part they may assume. The one class lacks that sympathetic nature which is the other's chief endowment, and while the public sits unmoved, but admiring, at the performance of the one, it is roused to enthusiasm at the impersonations of the other. The answer, then, to the question, What is the secret of dramatic success? would seem to be: Be born with this peculiar charm, and you will be able to awaken the sympathies of your audience. And, as no actor ever became great who had not the power to move the hearts of others, no study or perseverance can make up for this gift where Mother Nature has not been indulgent. Of course, devotion to one's art and arduous practice can make a man or a woman a good artist even when this great gift has been denied; but if one studies the characteristics of our great actors, past or present, one will find that their distinguishing feature is the degree in which they have possessed or do possess this indescribable something, which is very inadequately defined by some people as "personality."

In another place[1] I have written: Some people say that when you are acting upon the stage with an actor or actress you think they are good, and yet their art does not go "over the footlights" and reach the heart of the public. Sometimes I have been told, "How bad this actor is at rehearsal! and, close to you how unsympathetic, and yet what an effect he produces on his audience!" I do not believe this. I do not believe that any actor who is not sympathetic to act with—and by this I do not mean anything but actually the word I am using—sympathetic in his part—I say, I do not believe that such an actor's art *can* reach the public. If the tone of an actor's or actress's voice with whom you are acting does not allow you to answer them in the frame of mind and heart that you should be representing while you speak, and is not in sympathy with you, it is impossible for you to make the audience follow your train of thought. Acting is like photo-

[1] "Dramatic Opinions," by Mrs. Kendal. London: Murray, 1890.

graphy. One single person has instantaneously to photograph the same impression on the minds of hundreds. It is the duty of an actor to make the audience see the part from *his* point of view. If the audience is discussing whether the actor is right, the actor has not got hold of them. When I am acting, I must make the people feel that they see it from *my* point of view. If they discuss during the time I am acting whether I am right or wrong, I certainly have not got hold of them. They may discuss it afterwards, and say, "He was right," or "She was wrong"—this, that, and the other—but during the time I am acting it must be, as it were, a photograph thrown upon each individual mind of the audience, and I, or whoever is acting, must have the power to impress each mind so forcibly, that for the time at least it must see only the situation as it is so focussed.

This is one of the difficulties in playing a part taken from a well-known book. Each person among the audience, on reading the book, has drawn his own picture of the character. When they come to see an actor or an actress play that character, they immediately question whether it is right. "She did not do that. In the book I see so and so. He did not do so and so." Of course this difficulty is at its height when one is playing Shakespeare. It does great credit to the talent of the actor or actress if they realise to the *majority* the idea of the characters they have read of.

Madge Kendal

VI

MR. CYRIL MAUDE

THE successor of Mr. Beerbohm Tree in the management of the Haymarket Theatre is esteemed one of the very best comedians of the day, competent judges declaring him second only to Mr. Hare. Mr. Cyril Maude has certainly proved himself a thorough artist in everything he has done during his distinguished stage career, his great success in comedy having been no less pronounced in farce, modern drama, and old comedy. It was while a boy at Charterhouse School that Mr. Maude first developed his fondness for acting, and on his return home in 1881 from Australia, whither he had gone for the benefit of his health, he settled down in real earnest to study for the stage. But in the autumn of that year his health broke down again, and he went out to Canada, intending to try farming life for a time. He soon tired of this, however, and joining Daniel Bandmann's company at Denver, Colorado, he travelled the North-Western States, playing in all kinds of pieces, and seeing much queer life in those rough mining districts. In 1884 he came back to England, and played in a number of Criterion comedies on tour. Three years later his first London success was scored in "Racing," at the Grand, which led to a year's engagement at the Gaiety, and then two years at the Vaudeville. It was under the auspices of Mr. Thomas Thorne at this theatre that Mr. Maude gained some of his most valuable experience, and several of his most notable successes were obtained in the series of plays by Mr. Robert Buchanan, produced during Mr. Thorne's long and honourable management of the Vaudeville. Mr. Maude's wonderfully clever Hogarthian sketch of Lord Fellamar, in "Joseph's Sweetheart," was a notable performance, which proved what an artist the stage had secured in the young comedian; and his exquisite portrayal of Charles Farlow, in "That Doctor Cupid," will be fresh in the minds of all who saw it, now seven years ago. How realistic, how artistic, was every little touch of character!

His great success as Juxon Prall, in "Judah," followed shortly afterwards; but one of the very finest things he has done was his rendering of the polished cad, Philip O'Mara, in "Man and the Woman." The marvellous reality of the creation was the result of the artist's consummate skill and his close study of character. Then, what a convincing creation was his picture of the bounder, in "Meadow Sweet"! As one discerning critic has remarked, "There was character even in the turning up of the trousers." His Austin Woodville, in "Handfast," was also marked by the same keen observation and elaborate art, while a more finished study of decrepit old age was never placed on the stage than his performance in "Clarissa"; and his Duke of Mayfair, in "The Fringe of Society," was an equally noteworthy study of another and very different aspect of old age, Mr. Maude's picture of the aged reprobate being perfect. But Mr. Maude could scarcely fail to convince us in any new character he might assume by the method he pursues; possessing the artistic temperament in a marked degree, he goes direct to nature for his prototypes, and uses all the resources of his art to reproduce them on the stage.

Mr. Cyril Maude, like all artists who take a deep and abiding interest in their art, assures me that he is so conscious of what he has yet to learn himself that he hesitates before presuming to offer advice to others, and the opinions which he does venture to advance are set down with all humility in response to my queries. But it seems to me that Mr. Maude's opinions, which are to the following effect, are eminently worthy of publication:—

I beg to say that my methods of study are as follows: First of all, I always like to be present at the "reading" of the play, so that I may be enabled to form a really good idea of the piece, and of my own particular part. I also consider it desirable to hear all that is said by the other characters in the play concerning the character I have been called upon to impersonate, this being of great assistance in arriving at a proper estimate of my own part.

Then I commence the study in earnest, reading my part over and over again, and as soon as I feel that I have grasped the nature of the character, I prepare my "make-up" in accordance therewith, fix it on, and imagine in my own mind exactly the kind of man I have to represent. I also wander about London, looking for the particular type of man I want, so that my study may be modelled as close to nature as the exigencies of the stage permit.

I always make a point of knowing the "words" of my part if possible a fortnight before the production of the piece, but if this is not practicable, certainly a week before the first public performance. I never feel that I can do anything with a part until the words come trippingly off the tongue without any trouble, or hesitation; and I may here remark that I always write out my "cues" on pieces of note-paper which I carry about with me, taking them out of my pocket on every available occasion, and going through my part with their aid.

It is always my endeavour to present an entirely fresh type of man in each part I am cast for, and I strive to the utmost of my ability to play with a new voice and new manner, as well as with a new face. It may also be worthy of mention that I suffer intensely from nervousness at every first performance. This usually takes the form of dryness of the palate and throat, cramp in the hands and feet, and sickness.

Of course, in my own line of "business" the art of "making-up" is of vital importance. I find making-up exceedingly interesting work indeed, and it may interest readers to know that I usually take an hour to transform myself into the living picture of an old man.

As to the essentials of good acting, I scarcely know what to say, further than that concentration of thought and utter loss of self seem to me to be the first requisites of good acting: above all things, *clearness* of diction and *variety*. These words, "clearness and variety" might almost serve as a motto for stage aspirants. Another important thing is to always be "in the picture," and not to force one's self on the attention of the audience when that is not demanded by the nature of the situation. And, finally, need I say that one should not copy another actor's methods, but strive in every way to be original, except where there is tradition to follow?

Cyril Maude

VII

MR. CHARLES WARNER

Mr. Charles Warner, like so many distinguished players of the period, entered the dramatic profession with that aroma of romance which always clings to the deeds of runaway sons and revolted daughters. His parents, with that obtuseness which seems to be the distinguishing quality of all respectable parents, could not bear the thought of their son mixing with those vagrom men who wear the sock and buskin, and so young Charles, very much against his inclination, was sent to an architect's office, there to learn how to draw houses that are built of brick and mortar. But the stage fever, like murder, will out, and his ambition was firmly fixed upon the "drawing" of "houses" in the theatrical sense, and it is long since the height of that ambition was reached. Discarding the paternal shackles at the early age of seventeen, he threw his square and compass to the winds, and took to the stage, making his début in a stock-company at Hanley—one of those nightmare towns in the Potteries.

It has been alleged that during his stay at Hanley he played thirteen parts a week for eighteen shillings a week. While the first part of the allegation is very much overstated—as we shall presently hear, on the authority of Mr. Warner himself—it may be that the second is nearer the mark; for actors in small provincial stock-companies thirty years ago were remunerated more in experience than in filthy lucre. Mr. Warner obtained plenty of the one in his young days, and it is gratifying to know that he can command an abundance of the other nowadays. These two facts we may regard as cause and effect. But while Mr. Warner can claim the distinction of having earned one of the very largest salaries ever paid on the stage, he is too much of an enthusiast for the delightful art which he has followed so successfully to allow such materialistic considerations to influence him. A year at Hanley inspired him with sufficient confidence, as it had afforded him no little experience, to face "the town," and this he did as Romeo at the Princess's. Since then he has played many parts with that painstaking which always marks the true artist.

It has been Mr. Warner's misfortune to have his name so prominently identified with certain melodramatic characters that some people may have come to think of him only as Coupeau in "Drink," Tom Robinson in "Never too Late to Mend," Walter Lee in "Taken from Life," Ned Drayton in "In the Ranks," or Harry Dunstable in "A Million of Money"; but his claims to a prominent position in the very foremost rank of English actors of to-day are based, not merely on his wonderful impersonation of Coupeau, which part he has played such an unconscionable number of times, but on his acting in high comedy and legitimate drama. His Claude Melnotte is one of the finest we have seen, while in such parts as Harry Dornton, Charles Surface, Puff, and Charles Courtley, he is admirable.

Mr. Warner writes me as follows with reference to the

methods of study which he has found most advantageous, and would recommend to others:—

My advice to aspirants and young members of the dramatic profession is to study incessantly—Shakespeare for preference; but all the old dramatists. This course will widen, expand, and tremendously increase their desire for good and noble work, besides greatly improving their mind. As a youth I was an enthusiast; no part came amiss to me. I studied from morning until night, often until three A.M., besides attending to my ordinary work for the stage, which in my early career meant changing seven times a week. I found time to study such parts as Romeo, Mercutio, Othello, Richard III., Stranger, King John, Falconbridge, Hubert, Iago, Cassio, Shylock, Captain Absolute, and a host of other legitimate parts too numerous to mention.

At this time I was in my "teens," but my love for my profession was intense. I regret to say there is now no school for legitimate acting. Shakespeare is at a discount, and long runs, touring companies, &c., give the young actor but a poor chance to succeed in the higher range of drama. In my early career Mr. Phelps really had a school—the best and finest dramatic school in the world. I served my early London career under his banner, for three years at Drury Lane, playing in all the best legitimate and Shakespearian plays. Alas! no such educational course for the young actor now exists. But if the actor loves his profession, he will not neglect to study the great masters.

One important piece of advice to all who are contemplating a theatrical career: Let them pause and reflect. The stage is already overcrowded. I have seen good and sterling actors and actresses almost wanting bread. The rush for stage life lately has been immense, and only those who are endowed by nature with great dramatic gifts can hope to succeed. Therefore my advice is, weigh well the risks before taking the fatal step which will cut you off from a commercial career, and plunge you into all the uncertainties of a theatrical life.

VIII

MISS ELLEN TERRY

A DISCERNING critic has well said of Miss Ellen Terry that she is "mistress of the art of being natural." She is charming in an unconventional sense, she has all that magnetism, that subtle charm of personality which gives the great artist a firm hold over masses of people the most diversified tastes. Miss Terry comes of an old theatrical family, and has been on the stage since she was about nine years of age. Born at Coventry on the 27th of February 1848, she made her first appearance at the old Princess's Theatre, then under the spirited management of Charles Kean, playing Mamillius in "A Winter's Tale." She has told us how her heart swelled with pride when she learned what demands the part made upon her histrionic powers. "A small go-cart, which it was my duty to drag about the stage, was also a keen source of pride, and a great trouble to me. My first dramatic failure dates from that 'go-cart.' I was told to run about with it on the stage, and while carrying out my instructions with more vigour than discretion, tripped over the handle, and down I came on my back. A titter ran through the house, and I felt that my career as an actress was ruined for ever!" She later played Puck in "A Midsummer Night's Dream," which had a run of two hundred and fifty nights at the Princess's.

"I revelled in the impish unreason of the sprite," she says in an autobiographical note, "and even now feel the charm of parts where the imagination can have free play, and there is no occasion to observe too closely the cold, hard rules of conventionality and fetters of dry-as-dust realism."

When the Keans gave up management, Mr. Terry had a "Drawing-Room Entertainment" prepared for his promising daughters Kate and Ellen, and with this, which consisted of two separate little plays—"Distant Relations" and "Home for the Holidays"—the two youthful actresses, accompanied by their devoted father and mother, and Mr. Sydney Naylor, "who took the very important part of orchestra," toured the provinces with great success for three years. From the vein in which Miss Terry has subsequently written of this period in her career, it is evident she looks back upon it as one of the happiest she has ever experienced—and naturally so. Miss Ellen next appeared on the regular boards at the Royalty Theatre, in Dean Street, which had just been reopened under that name after having stood for years as the Soho Theatre. The manageress was a clever but eccentric little French lady, and she seems to have somewhat tried the young actress; but Miss Terry confesses that she profited by her experience at the Royalty.

After this she accepted an engagement with Mr. Chute's stock-company at Bristol, of which her sister Kate was already a member, and there she had as fellow-players Miss Madge Robertson (Mrs. Kendal), whose singing voice Miss Terry describes as being beautiful, Miss Henrietta Hodson (Mrs. Labouchere), Messrs. William and George Rignold, Mr. Coghlan, and others who have earned subsequent celebrity in the theatrical world. This Bristol engagement, she says, was excellent practice, as they played all things—tragedy, comedy, farce, and burlesque—her share being the second parts to her sister Kate—"Nerissa, Hero, and so forth in Shakespeare's plays, and all sorts of odds and ends in other plays." Returning to London she joined the Haymarket company, under Buckstone's management, playing Hero in "Much Ado about Nothing," Lady Touchwood in "The Belle's Stratagem," Julia in "The Rivals," and Mary Meredith in "Our American Cousin" ("somehow I could never like Mr. Sothern," she confesses), and yet she was only fifteen years of age!

Miss Ellen Terry was now fairly travelling the road to dramatic fame; in 1864, however, she married, and retired from the stage for a year. It was in December of 1867 that she first acted with Mr. Irving. The play was "The Taming of the Shrew," the theatre the Queen's. Miss Terry was the Katharina, and Mr. Irving the Petruchio. The old story that Mr. Irving was struck with her talent at the time, and promised that if he ever had a theatre of his own he would give her an engagement, she characterises as "moonshine." In the succeeding year she again withdrew from the stage, and did not reappear for six years, having, in the interim, married a second time. In 1878 the Lyceum passed into the hands of its present distinguished manager, who engaged Miss Terry as his leading lady, and eleven years after their first meeting they again appeared together, he as Hamlet, she as Ophelia. Stage history contains no brighter instance of the association of great dramatic talents than the intervening years have afforded us. Miss Ellen Terry has given to the stage a daughter and a son, Miss Ailsa Craig and Mr. Gordon Craig, both of whom show promise of brilliant dramatic gifts.

Through the kindness of Miss Ellen Terry I am able to publish the following expression of her opinions:—

Perhaps a word or two with reference to the dear old days when I, too, was a "beginner on the stage" may best illustrate my thoughts on the actor's apprenticeship. It was at the old Princess's that I was grounded in the essentials of an actress's education. Well do I remember the lessons in "deportment" which I received at the hands of dear old Mr. Byrn, the principal tenet of whose dramatic faith was that "an actress was *no* actress unless she had learned to dance early." He would have had walking and posturing reduced to an exact science. An old-fashioned minuet "step"—to which he attached especial importance—and, "walking the plank," which was to walk first slowly, then quicker, then at a considerable pace, along one of the planks extending the whole length of the stage, without deviating an inch from the straight line, were among his methods of giving an actress ease and grace in her actions. Although we children used to laugh at Mr. Byrn's military orders, I for one have since learned to appreciate the value, not only to deportment, but to a clear utterance, which lies in observing the order, "a chest thrown out, and a head thrown back."

In the most essential detail of articulation I learned much from Mrs. Kean even at this early period of my apprenticeship; for although that gifted actress mainly directed her instructions to the grown-up ladies of the company, I was always a willing pupil at her little lectures. "A, E, I, O, U, my dear," she used to say, "are five distinct vowels, so don't mix them all up together as if you were making a pudding. If you want to say 'I am going on the river,' say it plainly, and don't tell us you are going on the 'rivah'! You must say h*e*r, not h*a*r; it is G*o*d not G*u*d; rem*o*nstrance, not rem*u*nstrance," and so on. As to gesture she would say: "Use your arm from the shoulder, not from the elbow. Get your action free, don't stand like a trussed fowl." The value of such teaching when the mind is young and impressionable cannot well be overestimated. It has always seemed to me, however, that the best "school of acting" is the theatre, where students may go and witness good acting for themselves, with their eyes and ears open to the varying shades of expression, the propriety of actions, and interpretation of character.

I consider it is a very important thing that actors should at an early stage of their careers come under the influence of the immortal Shakespeare. The Shakespearian drama is the most wholesome of all food for the actor. During my juvenile days at the Princess's, that theatre was almost entirely given up to Shakespeare, and although I was very young then, I am conscious that, even as early as that, association with the Shakespearian drama was most beneficial to me, and the lessons learned almost unconsciously at the Princess's have, I am persuaded, been of no little use to me in my subsequent career.

One thing which the young actress must always bear in mind is, that no stage effects should be left to *chance*. Everything should be *rehearsed* and foreseen. No greater mistake is made than to suppose that because certain effects on the stage may seem to be spontaneous they are due to "the inspiration of the moment." The true artist always calculates to a nicety what he or she will do at certain crucial points in the progress of the play, and it is when the action thus prearranged is carried out with the appearance of spontaneity that the art is true. Seemingly accidental effects may thus be, and in a great artist always are, the result of much study and elaborate rehearsal. The beginner may regard the advice, "Always *act* at rehearsal," as one of the axioms of acting.

Another important thing is to have a *reason* for every action on the stage. Every movement, every look of the eye, should *tell* to some purpose; there should be no meaningless gesticulation. *Repose* is at once the most necessary and the most difficult thing to cultivate; but by perseverance the art of appearing at perfect ease under the critical gaze of an audience can be mastered.

IX

MR. LIONEL BROUGH

THIS favourite comedian, who is now in his sixtieth year, is the son of a dramatic author, Barnabas Brough, and a younger brother of Robert and William Brough, both well-known and popular writers for the stage in their time. In early life Mr. Brough was engaged in the office of the *Illustrated London News* during the editorship of Mr. John Timbs, and there he became acquainted with such famous people as Dickens, Thackeray, Jerrold, Leech, John Gilbert, and Albert Smith. Mr. Brough was subsequently assistant-publisher of the *Daily Telegraph* in its early days, and was next associated with the *Morning Star*, which has long since disappeared from the journalistic firmament. His dramatic début was made at the Lyceum, under the management of Madame Vestris and Charles Mathews, in "Prince Pretty Pet," one of W. Brough's burlesques, and "My Fellow Clerk"; but for some time he oscillated between the stage and newspaper publishing, latterly finding the attractions of the former irresistible. Mr. Brough's first engagement of importance in London was at the Queen's Theatre in 1866, when he appeared with Mr. Toole and Mr. Irving, as Ben Garner in Henry Byron's "Dearer than Life." His subsequent career has been one of practically uninterrupted success in comedy, farce, and burlesque. Mr. Brough is a comedian in the best sense of the word; no one ever played Bob Acres or Tony Lumpkin better.

I am afraid Mr. Brough has become such an inveterate humourist that he would find (if I may adapt an oft-quoted Shakespearianism) jokes in stones, quips in trees, laughter in the running brook, and fun in everything. But although he has written the following letter in cap and bells, the moral he would point is at once obvious and undeniable:—

I am hardly "in touch" with your book (he writes). I find the profession so overstocked with would-be actors, and being a prominent official on all our theatrical charities, I find so many of those persons on our funds, that I think a book which suggests methods of recruiting our already overstocked ranks might, instead of being a blessing, become a "curse." Every one thinks he can act, and looks upon any manager who does not engage him as a "crass ignoramus."

I remember a broken-down gentleman (?) who had tried the Stock Exchange, was afterwards a publisher, and failing in each he became a wine merchant. He next sold coals on commission, but meeting with no success in any of these avocations, he said—"I'm d—d if I shall not have to turn actor."

My theory is that—apart from the absolute necessity of possessing the requisite talent—to become an actor requires a long and arduous training, which can only be obtained by joining a company like that of Miss Thorne or Mr. Greet, where pieces are being continually changed, and where, by experience, a definite line of business may be determined upon.

No man or woman can become a capable member of our craft by merely playing one part in a long run, either in town or the provinces. They and their methods become identified with the one particular part they may have played—no matter with what success.

To be an actor or actress requires as much study and experience as is wanted for a doctor, a lawyer, or an artist. Thirty-five years' experience has shown me this.

Lionel Brough

NOTE.—I need only say, by way of comment to Mr. Brough's letter, that it would disturb my sleep o' nights if I thought the publication of this little work were calculated to add to the clamouring crowds already besieging the stage-door; but I think I am justified in expressing the belief that it is scarcely likely to tend in that direction. At any rate, it is by no means conceivable that a perusal of the opinions which I have been able to collect from men and women who have gone through the theatrical "mill" will induce the stage-struck youth, who thinks he can play Hamlet better, or at least as well, as Henry Irving, Beerbohm Tree, or Wilson Barrett, or the deluded maiden who would challenge comparison with Ellen Terry as Juliet, to seek admission to the ranks of a profession in which it is undeniable that success only comes after long years of patient drudgery and arduous study. And I am sure that Mr. Brough would be the last man to refuse a helping hand to the intelligent young man or woman who did really possess those sparks of dramatic fire which might, by careful tending, some day illumine the study of a character on the stage, and who was really prepared to accept all the initial hardships incident to the lower walks of the profession, in the hope that, by patient endeavour, he or she might attain to those loftier planes which are peopled by those who were once among the crowd at the stage-door. There are other points in Mr. Brough's communication upon which I might join issue with my genial correspondent, were it not that it has been my constant endeavour throughout these pages to subordinate my own opinions to those of people whom I consider more entitled to speak with authority, and, rather than pose as critic, I am content to assume the humbler office of compiler.

X

MR. HARRY NICHOLLS

THE 'prentice days of this genial comedian were spent in true Thespian fashion; for after a few months at clerking, when he was seventeen years of age he joined a fit-up company, and went touring round the "No. 3 towns," in which truly rural regions his experiences were varied, if not exciting. Even then, however, the artistic spirit was strong—perhaps even stronger than 'tis to-day;—and he confesses that there was at least one occasion on which he played to an audience of two in the pit. Only art for art's sake can afford such examples of professional altruism! The adventurous young actor, who was born in 1852, had received a good, sound education at the City of London School (where twenty-five years previously Mr. J. L. Toole had been a scholar), and being naturally gifted for the mimetic art, he soon made substantial progress in the profession he had entered by so humble a gateway. A couple of years of general "utility" in the provinces, at the magnificent salary of twenty-five shillings a week, and then he succeeded in obtaining an engagement as second low-comedian at the Surrey Theatre, where he remained until, in 1876, he migrated to the Grecian, to assume the leading low-comedy part in "Arrah-na-Pogue." This may be said to have been the turning-point in his career; for he soon became an established favourite, and four years afterwards the late Sir Augustus Harris secured him for Drury Lane, where, until recently, he was a continual source of attraction, both in pantomime and drama. He has latterly been appearing at the Adelphi. Mr. Nicholls has also written many of the best songs that have been sung in the music halls or on the burlesque stage during recent years, and he has been responsible for numerous provincial pantomimes, while he collaborated with the late manager of Drury Lane in the preparation of several of the Christmas annuals for the National Theatre.

It is a peculiar fact, but a fact none the less, that the philosopher is often to be found in motley, that the jester is the man to whom we have frequently to look for common-sense, if not, indeed, for some degree of wisdom. Thus, it is from Mr. Harry Nicholls that I have received one of the most philosophic—in a worldly sense, at least—of the letters that have been written in reply to my queries as to the best means of securing success on the stage.

I am afraid (writes Mr. Nicholls), I can be of very little assistance to you in the matter upon which you ask me to comment: there are so many ways of obtaining success on the stage—and so many ways of failing. Whatever of the former I have achieved has been due to the experience I gained during the first years of my professional life. Incessant study, constant rehearsals, continual change of pieces, supporting the "stars," and acting in every possible and impossible kind of play, from "Hamlet" to "Sweeney Todd," were the means by which I worked my way to the front.

Many, on the other hand, have attained popularity without any preliminary training (I am speaking now of some of the exponents of the lighter form of entertainment), to whom a knowledge of stage technique would have been a positive misfortune. But, after all, what does it matter? They are doing very well indeed, and if, like Polonius, they are accounted good actors, if the public is pleased, and good salaries are realised, then "Box and Cox are satisfied."

Harry Nicholls

XI

MADAME SARAH BERNHARDT

"WHEN leaving the convent at the age of fourteen, I remember I said, 'I shall either be a nun or an actress.'" Thus Madame Sarah Bernhardt. Fortunately for the stage—and equally fortunate for the veil, perhaps—the remarkable young woman became an actress, and a year after quitting the convent at Versailles, she entered the Conservatoire on the 29th November 1859. One of her teachers there was Provost, the master of Rachel, whose mantle has certainly descended to the shoulders of the divine Sarah. In 1861 she carried away the second prize for tragedy, and the next year she gained the second prize for comedy, these successes leading to her engagement at the Théâtre Français, where she appeared for the first time in "Iphigénie," without exciting any particular attention; but her appearance was not without result, as Montigny, the Director of the Gymnase, who had seen her perform, engaged her for *ingénue* parts. Her first part under his direction was in a *comédie bouffe*, and as it gave her nothing noteworthy to do except burst into frequent fits of laughter, she left, feeling that she could do something more dramatic than that—"and never went back." The girl was mother to the woman!

The young actress next appeared at the Porte Saint Martin, and, in 1866 she was employed at the Odéon, M. Duquesnel, who was convinced of her ability, engaging her at his own expense for one year, his colleague M. de Chilly refusing to be party to the engagement because he considered mademoiselle was too —thin! Her talent was placed beyond dispute during the time she remained at the Odéon—in all, six years; but it was not until she returned to the Comédie Française, in 1872, that she can be said to have scored a great success, her first real triumph being Phédre in Racine's famous tragedy. It is worthy of note that the opportunity, which in a stage career is almost as much as the ability, came to Madame Bernhardt by chance, the actress who was cast for Phédre refusing to play at the last moment. Since then "Madame Sarah"—as her friends are privileged to address her—has played in all parts of the civilised world; her fame has become universal. A woman of many activities, she is also a creature of strange impulses, but no one has ever questioned her genius. She can wield the sculptor's chisel with considerable success, the artist's brush and palette she uses to good advantage, and she has ventured into the domain of literature with encouraging results; but she is an actress first and last. She has often spoken her mind on her art, as indeed she does about most things that interest her, and a few of the opinions she has enunciated from time to time show that, though some of her ideas may be a trifle *outré*, her views of the art she follows are eminently sensible.

"For those young women who dream of success in a dramatic career," she says, "the absolute things indispensable are character, physique, and intelligence—a great deal of intelligence. To portray character it is necessary to have character, keen perception, and ready sympathy. All the faculties are called into play in the dramatic art; the higher the order of intelligence, the better suited is an artist to conceive a character or an emotion. The face must be capable of a wide range of expression. Physique is important — proportion, contour, outline. Taste in costuming does not make a good artist, but a good artist will show good taste in arraying herself, and the good sense to be guided in dressing by the epoch of the play. Grace is also absolutely important, and your woman with the artistic temperament will be graceful, for she has the innate artistic sense of what is beautiful and harmonious."

Speaking of how her effects are obtained, and in explanation of the means whereby she seeks to thoroughly identify herself with a personality on the stage, Madame Bernhardt says: "First of all, I study the intellectual composition of my rôle. I read every analysis and criticism of the character I can get hold of. If the character is historical, I read all the memoirs and biographies—every scrap of anecdote—all the legends of the poets. I saturate myself with the literature—the atmosphere of the epoch—until I feel that I am of it. I have a great gift of assimilation and intuition. If the artist cannot experience in actuality the sensations of the character she is portraying—be it sorrow, despair, or the pangs of agony or of death—she can give out the effect that the study of any or all these have had on her intelligence and sensibility; and by the degree of her sensibility is determined the greatness of her representation. The Latin orator was right, 'It is the heart and the vivacity of intelligence that render eloquent'; and from me," she goes on to say, "extends an influence of sensibility which on the fiftieth—the hundredth night of one of my rôles communicates to the spectators *un frisson particulier*. Sometimes the situation may exalt me, or the state of my nerves—or some personal souvenir of remembrance—may cause me to rise to a still greater height, or predispose me to a more intense sincerity. But, you have seen me playing to audiences knowing but little French; yet, wherever I go, the public always understand me. Then, I am always studying character. Every one I meet is a new study. I am always studying people!"

Like Betterton, Siddons, and many other great actors past and present, Madame Bernhardt is often dressed an hour before she is due on the stage, and, sitting in her room, she exercises that subtle gift of introspection and mental concentration which is the most important element of the artistic temperament, and is thus *en rapport* with her assumed character before she steps upon the stage. "I am always nervous," she confesses, "because I am always afraid of falling below my previous standard of acting. I have met with unsympathetic audiences in my time, but I don't know that an unsympathetic audience has much effect on me. I am not sure that I don't rather enjoy it for a change, for it is then a battle between me and them, and I always win!"

On the important subject of dress the famous tragedienne says: "I have a great horror of shams on the stage—of what will not bear close inspection—of what is not real. I never use spangles, tinsel, and cheap theatrical glitter—it offends my artistic sense. I always employ hand embroideries in bullion and silk, and will have nothing to do with the generally used *appliqué* embroideries on the stage, and I have found that what *is* best always has the best effect, whether looked at from a distance or near at hand. My freedom of movement, the lightness of my step, the suppleness and flexibility of my body, I attribute to having definitely abandoned the corset, for an actress should wear nothing that is calculated to hamper and impede her movements."

As an evidence of the great care which Madame Bernhardt devotes to her costuming, it may be added that her *couturier* is not alone the author of her dresses, as she herself has much to do with the making of them. "I select the design," she says, "and then give orders as to the form and general arrangements. The modelling and draping I do for myself, and then I take a great pair of scissors and make all the alterations that appear to me requisite. Sometimes I wear a new costume for a number of rehearsals with the material only pinned together, and will not allow a stitch to be put in it until it falls softly and becomes quite moulded to the lines of my figure."

On the art of making-up Madame Bernhardt writes: "Not even after I had gone on the stage did I receive any instruction in a branch of art on which many actors lay great stress. I was permitted to experiment for myself and find out by observation and experience. I fear that at first I sadly overdid the matter. I was extravagant in the use of rouge, and powder, and black, and blue. As time wore on I came to regard these aids less highly. Expression became more, and make-up less. Dry rouge, rice-powder, and one or two pencils, give me all the effect I require. As with most artists, my first application is a liberal coat of cold-cream. This is made under my own immediate care, and consists of refined olive-oil, rose, water, and *blanc de baleine.* I never use cocoa-butter, nor liquid preparations of any sort. Then the pencils, the rouge, and the powder are applied, and all blended in to produce the effect of smoothness.

"With French artists, quite as much attention is given to the ears, the nostrils, and the lips, as to the complexion itself. For the lips is used a simple preparation which carries nothing but the carmine colouring matter. This is a brilliant colour, necessarily so to give the contrast to the exaggerated tints of the rest of the face. Depending upon the character of the emotion to be depicted in different plays, and even in different acts of the same play, the usual changes I make are only in the varying proportions of red to white. As I never wear a wig, the only way in which I make up my hair is to dress it appropriately to my costume and the period it represents. I do not think any artist ever secured greatness by the use of make-up, and the natural good looks of many actresses are spoiled both on the stage and off by employing cosmetics too freely."

XII

MR. HARRY PAULTON

ACQUIRING fame as a delightful low-comedian, and for long the favourite of Alhambra audiences, Mr. Harry Paulton's latter-day histrionic successes have been won in comedy parts. He was born at Wolverhampton in 1843, and—how often must we write the phrase?—was, in his teens, a most enthusiastic amateur. But he was more than enthusiastic—he was clever and successful; making quite a hit, from an amateur's point of view, in private theatricals when he was nineteen years of age. He seems to have gone on the lines which Mr. Toole lays down in his contribution to the present work; for, finding that his amateur efforts were favourably received, that his friends were interested and not bored by his performances, he set his face towards the stage, and in 1865 he found himself across the frontier of that fascinating land which lies behind the great plush curtain, and is irradiated by means of the footlights. Working hard for the next five years in various parts of the provinces, he laid in that store of experience which is legitimately the boast of every actor whose early days were spent in stock-companies. Mr. Paulton soon became a favourite with provincial audiences, and his London chance came in good time, when, in 1870, he was engaged to play the part of Blueskin in "The

Idle Apprentice," at the Strand Theatre, with which playhouse his subsequent fame and fortune have been closely associated.

Mr. Paulton met with very gratifying success on coming to London, first in comedy parts, but subsequently his name had become so popularly identified with successful low-comedy creations that when, in 1892, he again assumed a comedy part in "The Parvenu," at the Globe, the world of playgoers was surprised, but not disappointed. For Mr. Paulton has proved himself a past master both in comedy and low-comedy. Meanwhile he had ventured into the domain of dramatic composition with the happiest results. He was part author of "The Black Crook," which was produced very successfully at the Alhambra, and met with even greater success across the Atlantic. In 1883 his play, "Cymbria," was the attraction at the Strand for some time, and the following year he produced that delightful extravaganza, "The Babes; or, W(h)ines from the Wood," which ran at Toole's for over a hundred nights, and in which Miss Alice Atherton made her memorable hit. "The Babes" was revived at the Strand in February 1895 by Mr. Willie Edouin, with Miss Atherton in her old part. In 1885 "Erminie," the successful comic opera, appeared, and of this Mr. Paulton was the joint-author, next collaborating with his brother in the construction of "Niobe (All Smiles)," which enjoyed such a remarkable run at the Strand Theatre, and which is still a potent attraction in the provinces. "Dorcas," a bright little comedy-opera, is one of his later productions, and in it he has recently been renewing acquaintances with his provincial friends.

Mr. Paulton has been good enough to respond to my request by writing the following interesting article on the Art of Acting:—

I write of the "art of acting," for acting appears to have been definitely raised to that dignity, within recent years at all events. When, a few years back, the point was seriously discussed there were dissentient voices, even among the followers of "the" profession, as a popular journal will persistently, and, I am afraid, scoffingly, have it. But opposition to the actor's claims to be considered an artist eventually died out; no one now offers, or enters, any protest, and we may, presumably, take it for granted that acting is an art.

The art of acting, however, differs materially from other arts, and this chiefly from, what at first may sound like a startling statement—the fact that *it does not require to be taught.* Providing a man has the natural aptitude and the latent ability, all that is necessary to make him an actor is experience and practice. And here it is scarcely necessary to remark that no amount of practice or experience will make an actor out of a man who does not possess "the right stuff." I have met those whom neither experience nor anything else would ever have turned into actors. But I confidently assert that, given sufficient experience, the aspirant who is naturally fitted for the work will make an actor of himself.

It is in this respect, I think, where acting differs essentially from other arts. It is this which always makes the talk of "schools of acting" sound like so much twaddle and nonsense in my ears. If those who advocate these can establish and run successfully a theatre where plays of all sorts, and "plenty of 'em," may be performed, and call *that* their "school," then I am with them.

Personally, I never received a lesson in acting in my life; and by that I mean a lesson in the sense that a tutor instructed me to "do this so," or "that the other way"; but in the continual lesson of playing many parts, to a great extent in *one's own way*, and so finding out one's own strength and weakness, Yes.

In the old stock days a stage-manager never attempted to teach acting. He would correct a palpably wrong reading or a mispronunciation: he would tell you if you came on Right or Left, on which side you stood, where you crossed; but little more. You were supposed to be an actor, and you played small parts, wherein little was expected from you, until practice brought proficiency, and then you moved up. This, in my opinion, was the proper kind of schooling.

Mimicry is not acting. A very excellent mimic may be a vile actor. I can recall instances, one in particular, of an actor, somewhat celebrated in his time, whom I have seen imitate Kean, Phelps, or Fechter, with all the finish and ease of these celebrated tragedians, in bearing and in action, and half an hour afterwards, playing a part "on his own," he would be in obvious distress as to how to move about the stage, or where to put his hands.

But in all that I have said, I do not mean to infer that much valuable instruction cannot be imparted, that many useful hints cannot be given. The beginner will be wonderfully assisted by useful advice from the experienced; but my opinion is, that without actual practice—acting to *an audience*—he will hardly become an actor. Music and painting may have their schools, and there is, perhaps, no other way of promulgating the knowledge of these arts. In a school of painting the pupil is set to draw and then to paint. He takes his brushes and pigments, with these he paints, very badly, perhaps, at first, but with instruction and practice, trying and failing, and improving, unless he has completely mistaken his vocation, he in time becomes an adept. With music it is precisely the same. The pupil sings or plays scales or exercises, poorly and indifferently, till tuition, with incessant practice, perfects him.

In the case of acting, experience and actual work outweigh everything, "always and providing" the young actor or actress has the natural aptitude. The person who has played a hundred parts will be a better actor than the one who has had a thousand lessons.

XIII

MR. LAWRENCE IRVING

THE son of a famous man always starts his public career at a distinct disadvantage. The world, to use a common phrase, expects him to begin where his father leaves off. But Mr. Lawrence Irving has already proved himself the gifted son of a gifted sire, and young as he is to the stage, he has given us something more than the mere promise of future attainments. Born on 21st December 1871, the second son of Sir Henry Irving was educated at Marlborough College, and was intended for the Diplomatic Service. With this end in view he was sent to be educated in Paris, and on leaving school there in 1887, he went to Russia, where he spent three years. But, as was inevitable, Mr. Irving had always had a liking for theatricals, and one of his most noteworthy performances during his stay in the capital of the Czar was to organise a dramatic entertainment—the first ever given there in the English language—in aid of the Imperial Conservatoire of Music. The success of this performance must have been unqualified, as Mr. Irving was able to hand over to the Conservatoire no less a sum than £200 towards its funds. His own histrionic efforts on this occasion were very highly praised by competent judges, and it is not surprising that soon afterwards the embryo diplomatist began to develop in another direction—to turn his eyes towards the stage and away from despatch boxes and sealing-wax. Indeed, we might be correct in saying that the greatest service he ever rendered the diplomatic relationship of Russia and England was his dramatic performance in aid of the Imperial Conservatoire of Music. It is the old story of "What's bred in the bone" over again. How few are the instances in which great actors have been able to prevent their children, strive how they may, from taking to the stage! Nine out of every ten actors to-day—yesterday, and to-morrow, for that matter—were "intended" for the bar, the ministry, politics, journalism, art, or any other calling under the sun but acting. And so, in Mr. Lawrence Irving and his brother Harry, the stage has gained what diplomacy and the law have lost, and all lovers of the stage will agree that it would have been a thousand pities had either of these rather prosaic professions absorbed two brilliant young men, who were as naturally fitted for the stage as ducklings for a pond.

When Mr. Lawrence Irving returned to England in 1890, resolved to test his fortunes on the stage, he set about studying in earnest for the art which he had elected to follow, and his first public appearance on the professional boards was made under the ægis of Mr. F. R. Benson at Dundee, in August 1891, when he assumed the part of Snug the Joiner in Mr. Benson's excellent production of "A Midsummer Night's Dream." He remained with Mr. Benson's Shakespearian Company till January 1892, gaining that valuable experience which is now only to be had in playing a round of parts in a first-class repertoire company. Paris, Lorenzo, Nym, Osric, and Conrad were among the characters in which he appeared during his initial provincial season, and his success was so pronounced that immediately after his short probation Mr. Toole engaged him to appear in

"Daisy's Escape," at his famous old theatre, which has recently been demolished. Mr. Irving subsequently toured the provinces with Mr. Toole in "Walker, London," his clever impersonation of Andrew McPhail introducing him to provincial playgoers as a character comedian, in which "line" Mr. Ben Greet, under whose auspices the young actor has accomplished some excellent work, considers he is destined to achieve greatness. Mr. Irving, young as he is, has also been an actor-manager, and his own provincial tour with "The Lady of Lyons," "Silas Ruthven" (written by himself in collaboration with Mr. Seymour Hicks), and other plays, was very successful, while lately he has performed Svengali in Mr. Abud's production of "Trilby" in all the important provincial towns. His talent for dramatic composition bids fair to rival his gift of dramatic expression, though it is rarely we find the two combined in the one individual. His "Silas Ruthven" showed considerable promise; but this, we are told, has been more than fulfilled in a very remarkable short play of his, in which Miss Ellen Terry achieved a great success during the last American tour of the Lyceum Company, and which will, we hope, be seen in London some of these days. And Mr. Irving's wedding gift to his brother's wife, Miss Dorothea Baird, the incomparable Trilby, included an original play from his pen, in which, no doubt, that charming actress may appear some day. Thus, his five years of the stage have not only been full of promise, but remarkable in performance; indeed, a stronger case of hereditary talent could not be cited, and there can be no doubt that Mr. Lawrence Irving is fairly launched on a brilliant dramatic career.

Mr. Irving sends me the following contribution, embodying his views on the art of acting and the actor's apprenticeship:—

In my short experience—for, according to the best qualified opinions, it takes a man of average capacity from thirty to fifty years (a decade more or less counts for little or nothing in an estimate of this kind; you may expand or contract the quantity of years according to your age and your achieved position) to become a veritable and, if I may be allowed the expression, a verifiable actor—in my short experience, then, I have evolved three simple little maxims for my guidance. These are: First, make up your mind; second, precede speech by action, and action by expression (facial); third, profit only by your own experience.

"Make up your mind."—If, at the very outset, an aspirant (I believe this is the most respectful appellation), on being taken through any part whatsoever—provided it is a character and not a mere lay figure—shows a clear want of capacity for co-ordinating ideas out of the slight suggestions of the written text, that man, in my opinion, will never become an actor. I do not say he will never achieve success on the stage; I do not say he will never taste the joys of "starring," of laying foundation stones, and so forth. Oh, dear no! I merely say that he will never become an actor. But, then, what do I really know about it? Little or nothing! Is it not a notorious fact that every young aspirant very properly and rightly believes that *he* is *the* destined actor? The lapse of years usually diminishes somewhat this self-assurance; and, therefore, if you discover any arrogance in the tone or method of laying down my half-fledged opinions, set it to me, if you please, for modesty and a confession of incompetence.

In studying a part, one should not, I fancy, evoke the conditions of actual presentation; but one should, in one's mind's eye, reinstate that fourth wall, or that view of the distant hill-tops—whichever the case may be. So may one hope to avoid the pitfalls of staginess, and counteract the insidious counsel of the "blind old actor," who never hesitates to lead the one-eyed novice into these very pitfalls. One should always be wary of what is comparatively easy of acquisition—stage trick, &c. But one should hold tenaciously to what one has elicited out of one's self by dint of persevering study. I say "hold tenaciously," because, although the art of acting is essentially one of give-and-take, the "blind old actor" has misconstrued this proposition into meaning that he does all the taking and the "one-eyed novice" all the giving. And may I be permitted, as one of the novices myself, to offer to the others of my kind the following receipt for the treatment of the aforesaid "blind old actor"? If that individual pester you with offers of advice, appease him by the loan of your face paints; if he pester you still, offer him your best curled wig; if he pester you further, lend him a shilling; and if after all he pester you still, ask him to pay you back. I answer for the efficacy of this treatment.

If you take the trouble, which I do not think you will, to look back at the commencement of this paper, you will see that I started with the intention of discussing each one of my three simple little maxims in order, but from lack of system, I have utterly failed to do so. I have allowed myself to be drawn aside from the higher questions involved by the necessity for relief—comic, if possible. Therefore I shall just continue on at random, noting things down as they occur to me.

After all is said and done, who ever derived any assistance in the practice of an art from its theory? And what does all this theory mean? Simply this: twice two is four, and the component parts of two are one and one. Be born an actor and you will become one. Earnestness and obvious enthusiasm are the symptoms of inexperience. They are intolerable in a small dressing-room; and if they are not obtrusive, they are other qualities than those I mean. For no more can a drilled soldier return to his former state of country bumpkin, than earnestness and enthusiasm consider suitability or expediency.

But I begin to feel that I have cut away the ground from under my own feet by just now admitting the uselessness of theory. In fact, at the very outset, did I not lay down as my third simple little maxim, "Profit only by your own experience"? This clearly annuls all that has gone before and renders me guilty of the most obvious futility. My only consolation is that I err in such excellent company. So now, ye eager aspirants, *au revoir!* Yes, we shall meet there—in the dressing-room—on the stage! Why not follow up all that money you have spent on paints and powders, "Stages," and "Eras"? You ought to do so. Satisfy yourselves. Take no one's word for anything. And—*au revoir!*

XIV

MISS GENEVIÈVE WARD

THIS talented and experienced actress is an American by birth, having been born in New York, her father being Colonel Samuel Ward, and her mother a daughter of Gideon Lee, a mayor of the Empire city. Mrs. Ward was a lady of marked artistic attainments, and when the family removed to Paris, her salon there was attended by many of the intellectual giants of the time—Horace Vernet, Balzac, Alfred de Musset, and others. Thus, the future actress was early brought into association with ideals of art, and her refined up-bringing had much to do in shaping her subsequent artistic career. Her early years also held a romance for her, as she was married to a Russian nobleman, Count Constantine de Guerbel, and by a remarkable chain of events parted from him at the hymeneal altar for ever. Soon afterwards she devoted herself to music, and assuming the name of Madame de Guerrabella, made her début in London at the Philharmonic concerts in Hanover Square, appearing later on the lyric stage at Her Majesty's Opera, with Titiens and other celebrated artistes. While on an operatic tour in that other distressful island, Cuba, Madame de Guerrabella lost her singing voice through overwork, and so she turned her attention to music-teaching in New York. Six months of this drudgery was sufficient for her, and having commenced in earnest to study for the dramatic stage, she returned in 1873 to London, where she was offered an engagement in pantomime, and then one in farce! But her fixed purpose was tragedy, and the spirit in which these magnanimous offers were received—or rather rejected—by the future tragedienne can easily be imagined.

Through the good offices of the late Lewis Wingfield she obtained a hearing in a recital of "Macbeth," and this happily led to an engagement at Manchester, where Miss Ward—for about this time she resumed her maiden name—appeared with encouraging success as Lady Macbeth, and afterwards as Constance. She next performed in Dublin as Media, Adrienne, and Lucrezia Borgia, and coming back to London, in 1874, she succeeded Miss Wallis at the Adelphi, shortly afterwards appearing at Drury Lane. Her reputation was now fairly established, and Miss Ward was able to satisfy her artistic sense by arranging a tour in the Shakespearian drama. But she was too much an artist to suppose that her training was anything like over, and proceeding to Paris she studied French tragedy and comedy under Regnier. Back in England again she played with Charles Calvert in "Henry VIII.," and subsequently went out to America with a company of her own. When she again returned to London Miss Ward boldly entered upon all the risks of management at the Lyceum, where she produced Palgrave Simpson's "Zillah," and though that was by no means successful, her production of "Forget-me-Not" was a memorable triumph. Since then Miss Ward has always been busy at her profession, unswerving in her devotion to the highest ideals of the dramatic art, either in London, America, or the Colonies, and more recently she has been one of the chief attractions in Sir Henry Irving's Lyceum company. An artist of abiding merit, she has been eulogised by no less a personage than the poet Longfellow in these words: "She is the greatest actress I have ever seen, and quite the most artistically faultless."

Miss Geneviève Ward writes me to the following effect:—

What are the essentials of good acting and the qualities of a good actor? The question is easily asked, but less easily answered. Indeed, it cannot be answered satisfactorily in the small compass of a letter, nor in the time at my disposal. The subject is a wide one, and may well furnish forth material for a bulky volume. Suffice it for me to state, that in my opinion the physical attributes of an actor or actress—and these are of great, if not supreme, importance—should be a good figure, an expressive face, clear, sonorous, penetrative voice, articulation distinct and unhesitating, and a graceful bearing. Mentally he or she should be endowed with a keen perception of character, artistic tastes, and above all, the *dramatic instinct.*

By dramatic instinct I mean that natural quality which enables one almost intuitively to simulate the effects produced by the various emotions and passions on the human creature, and to understand the workings of these emotions. This inborn power of controlling the means employed for the simulation of these emotions is the *sine quâ non* in every great actor, or in any one who would seek by "action and utterance and the power of speech to move men's hearts." The method to be used in mastering these means will vary with the individual student; and the only certain formula I can name is *work* and *observation.*

As well as all the qualities I have enumerated the

would-be actor or actress must have a persevering industry, without which ultimate and permanent success is not attainable. In addition to great natural gifts, all who have reached eminence on the stage of the past or the present have had this capacity for constant and untiring industry. "There are no gains without pains."

On the question of emotion, and as to whether an actress should "feel" her part, I cannot do better, perhaps, than recall the remarks I contributed some years ago to Mr. Archer's symposium on "The Psychology of Acting." Tears always come to my eyes in a moving situation, but seldom run over. Sometimes they are unbidden, and sometimes I work up to them. I have been obliged when studying a part (Constance in "King John," for instance) to stop owing to tears and sobs, and would not have attempted to play it until I could control my feelings. I find that I feel much more when alone than before an audience; then I must make them feel—control myself to control them. I have not found it made any difference with my audience whether I actually shed tears or not—very few *see* the real tear—they *feel* the pathos of the situation and do a good part of the acting themselves.

I must confess that I am somewhat doubtful as to the artistic value of personal emotion; but I have no such doubt as to its tendency to mingle with the emotion of the scene. Many sad experiences in my life have helped to intensify my feelings on the stage, even though not strictly analogous; but I have not found that it made any difference in the effect upon my audience. The influence on myself was to make me suffer, not only from the sorrow, but from the effort to control my feelings and keep them within the bounds of the situation. I have seen a young actress, whose pathos rarely touched her audience, perform one night under the influence of the deepest sorrow, tears rolling down her cheeks freely, and sobs breaking her voice. Yet the audience was quite as unmoved as on other occasions in the same situation. This, to my mind, proves that personal emotion, unaccompanied by the power of dramatic expression, is not sufficient to move an audience.

Geneviève Ward

XV

MR. ACTON BOND

THE real hope of the stage are those younger actors who not only possess genuine dramatic talent, but are earnest followers of their art, studious and sincere in all the work they get to do. Such an one is Mr. Acton Bond, who was born in Toronto, and made his first professional appearance at the St. James's Theatre in Messrs. Hare and Kendal's revival of "Clancarty," playing the small part of Officer of the Guard. Prior to this, however, Mr. Bond had played a variety of parts as an amateur and semi-professional; was cast for the part of the Bleeding Sergeant in "Macbeth" at the special performance in which Mr. Willard appeared as Macbeth and Mrs. Bandmann-Palmer as Lady Macbeth at the old Olympic Theatre. After two or three matinées of unimportant new plays, Mr. Bond joined Mr. Osmond Tearle for a year's work in the "legitimate," during which time he played some thirty parts, including "juvenile," "heavy," comedy, and "old men," being released just before the end of the tour to accept an engagement with Mrs. Bandmann-Palmer as Harry Blakiston in "Tares." He next played Robert Ffolliot in the "Shaughraun," for Messrs. Howard and Wyndham, the well-known Glasgow managers, then "on tour" for three months, playing light comedy in "Arabian Nights," and Mr. Grundy's "Man Proposes." An engagement to play the title rôle in "The Silver King" followed, and for fifty nights Mr. Bond appeared in that part in the provinces, his next engagement being for Mr. William Terriss's special production of "Harbour Lights" at the Grand Theatre, in which he undertook the part of Frank Moreland. This was succeeded by a summer season at Drury Lane, Mr. Bond there playing General Kletere in "Paul Kauvar," then another special engagement with Mr. Terriss as Colonel La Hogue in the same piece, and light comedy in "The Rough Diamond." He afterwards toured for three months, appearing in the dual rôles of Lucien Laroque and Luversan in "A Man's Shadow"; was the Lord Maidment during the run of "The Bookmaker" at the Globe, and had appeared in a number of characters at matinées, and was professionally retained by the Browning Society for the principal part, Djabal, in Browning's "Return of the Druses," before he joined the Lyceum company in January 1892.

He remained with Mr. Henry Irving until July 1893, playing Surveyor to Buckingham in "Henry VIII.," the Duke of Orleans in "Richelieu," Robin Hood in Lord Tennyson's poetical play "The Foresters," King of France and Duke of Burgundy in "King Lear," and King Louis of France in Tennyson's "Becket," in which character he had the honour of performing before Her Majesty at Windsor Castle, when the piece was produced there by special command. Mr. Bond did not accompany the Lyceum company to America in 1893, and referring to this in an interview with a representative of the *Era*, he said: "It seems to me that a young actor never quite realises the actuality of his art until he has been through two or three productions under Henry Irving. Everything is done so beautifully there that it appears absolutely real; one lives in the very atmosphere of the time depicted. I think, however, that if one cherishes the ambition for personal triumphs as an actor, an unbroken time at the Lyceum Theatre would not be advantageous. One should go elsewhere while the precepts of the great leader of our profession are still vital, and the endeavour to work on one's own responsibility in his spirit ought not to fail to have the best results." The first thing Mr. Bond played after leaving the Lyceum was the leading part in Michael Field's tragedy, "A Question of Memory," at the Independent Theatre, and he has since sustained principal parts in many notable productions, playing with Miss Elizabeth Robins the leading rôles in the special performances of "The Master Builder" and "Hedda Gabler" at Manchester. He was also the Paris on the occasion of the very successful matinée when Miss Esmé Beringer appeared as Romeo and Miss Vera Beringer as Juliet, and subsequently appeared at the Gaiety with Miss Olga Nethersole in "Carmen." Mr. Bond's last big part was Othello.

At my suggestion Mr. Acton Bond has written the appended article embodying his opinions of the art:—

I would put at the beginning of my remarks the importance of finding some effective means of testing the suitability of stage recruits; for it is imperative that something should be done in order to stop the overcrowding of our profession by incompetent people—an evil which is recognised and regretted on all hands. A great deal might be done in the direction indicated if all aspirants could be subjected to a preliminary examination before they were allowed either to commence training or—as is generally the way nowadays—to join a company for small parts. I feel very strongly this need for stopping the increase of incompetent actors, as much in their own interests as in those of the drama. Under the present haphazard system—or want of system, rather—people of no real dramatic talent are continually going on the stage, the first work being comparatively easy, and such as any person of ordinary intelligence may perform; but they can't continue in those little parts all their lives, and so they are soon among the claimants for better work, and here it is that their incompetence becomes so painfully evident.

Any examination such as I suggest need not be *very* severe, but it ought to be stiff enough to discover whether the aspiring Irvings and Ellen Terrys possess any degree of the necessary dramatic instinct, and the capacity for giving that expression, even crude and undeveloped though it might be. If some such plan as this were followed it would result in freeing the stage of the absolute duffers, and that is a consummation devoutly to be wished. I might here mention that I have particularly noticed on many occasions, when acting as judge at dramatic competitions, that had some kind of entrance examination been enforced, *at least one-third* of the competitors would not have been allowed to commence at all.

When the right material has been discovered I recommend a course of coaching in modern and legitimate parts; fencing if possible; and certainly instruction in the development and proper use of the voice. Many otherwise excellent actors fail in a part because of their inability to make themselves clearly and distinctly heard; when a part demands sustained voice power, then for want of knowing how to use it properly the voice gives out at the critical moment. My contention is, that the voice should be so trained and practised that it may become like an organ, capable of being played on at will. Most voices require, and ought to get, almost daily practice, in order that they may become of the greatest value to their possessors; for, in my opinion, the voice plays a vital part in the ultimate success of the actor. I would go so far as to say, that even when playing regularly, voice practice of a different kind to the evening work is essential.

One must be personal occasionally to help one's arguments, and so I venture a word or two as to my own experience. Shortly after I had commenced stage work professionally I was lucky enough to be with Mr. Osmond Tearle for a year. The continual round of parts of all kinds, and the work generally in which I then engaged, has been of great help to me since, not only personally, but when I am training others. That is why I suggest that beginners could not do better than endeavour to join a good repertoire company, such as those of Mr. Osmond Tearle, Mr. F. R. Benson, Mr. Edward Compton, and Mr. Ben Greet, names which come readily to my mind. An engagement under any of these gentlemen is of itself a splendid experience; though, even if the beginner has the good fortune to be admitted into one of these companies, I still think a preliminary coaching would be of great advantage.

My method of studying a part is, I should imagine, the general one; but as you ask for a word or two on this point, I shall endeavour to explain, as briefly as possible, my way of treating a part. My first concern, of course, is to endeavour to arrive at a true estimate of the character of the part, and to get the whole scheme of the play into my head, noting particularly how the man I am to represent stands in juxtaposition to the other characters. Then I commence to study the words, and as the words become familiar, I polish my conception of the character until I gradually come to live the man in thought, and almost in action.

While on this subject I would like to say how I deplore the fact, that actors are governed so much by precedent in respect to the parts that they may play.

When one has been playing leading parts long enough to be recognised as a leading man, if he, for the purpose of bringing the necessary grist to the inexorable mill, were to play an old man's part, he would find it a difficult matter to make managers understand that he had not thus made a permanent change, but had merely accepted the part as an interlude between one leading part and the wait for the next. These absurd precedents seem to me to be most objectionable; an actor should be at liberty to play in any kind of part without so damaging his future career—always providing, of course, that he played his part well.

Another point I would like to note, namely, the tendency to cast blame on the actor, or what some consider even worse, to ignore him, when he is filling a bad part in a bad play. It would be equally as just to disparage a barrister when defending a hopelessly bad case. The actor sometimes plays a bad part because he has to earn his living, and the barrister defends a hopeless case for precisely the same reason. Let us be judged by the work we do if it is earnest, whether the part be good or bad. Naturally we all prefer good parts in good plays, but these are not always to be had, and all that I claim is that the actor should receive due consideration when he has to perform unsatisfactory work. We have to remember it is necessary to live and pay our way.

Acton Bond

XVI

MR. WEEDON GROSSMITH

Mr. Weedon Grossmith is that *rara avis*, an actor who, in his young days, had a distinct disinclination to the stage. And his father, the George Grossmith of a former generation, actually urged him to become an actor! Why, it sounds impossible; but there is no reason to doubt that it is a fact. Mr. Weedon Grossmith—who everybody knows is the brother of George of that ilk—was devoted to Art when a young man, exhibited at the Academy in 1880, and met with some success as a portrait painter. But after a time he became discontented with the profession he had chosen, and began to think of trying his fortune on the stage. So, in 1885, he accepted an offer of a two years' engagement in the United States, for the purpose of gaining confidence and experience. He was very successful, and became such a favourite in America that he might have remained there had the climate been more suited to his health.

Coming back to London he appeared at the Gaiety in October 1887, and in the summer of the next year he made a hit at the Lyceum, with Mr. Irving, as Jacques Strop in "Robert Macaire." He was next with Mr. Richard Mansfield at the Globe, then with Mr. Beerbohm Tree, and he really made his mark as the little Hebrew money-lender, Joseph Lebanon, in "The Cabinet Minister," which was produced on 23rd April 1890. Subsequently at the Court he appeared in several amusing pieces, becoming an immense favourite as Lord Arthur Pomery in that diverting skit, "A Pantomime Rehearsal," in which he had appeared during his two years in America. His tenure of management at the Vaudeville was most successful, and in "The New Boy" he was lucky enough to find a little Bonanza. Success has dogged his footsteps since the day he took to the stage, and yet he wanted to be a painter! But he occupies his leisure to some purpose with the brush and palette.

In the course of a letter to me Mr. Grossmith writes:—

You must really excuse my not writing about the art of acting, because I—I *cannot* state my opinions on the subject! The fact of the matter is, I cannot give my views to be put in print and everlastingly brought up "as evidence against me." *Ergo*, my discretion tutors me to preserve silence on this point. All that I can say as to the learning of a part is that it causes me no end of trouble. It is the most difficult thing I ever have to do. When studying a new part I will wander about back streets for hours on end, with a little book in my hand, which I have copied the words into. I will go round my garden dozens of times, repeating the words over and over again, and trying to get myself into the frame of mind they suggest. I will ride in trains, getting a carriage to myself, where I may spout away to my heart's content, and, perhaps best of all, I will get into a four-wheel cab, telling Jehu to drive anywhere he likes for an hour or so, and there I will contrive to forget everything but my part for the time being, and immerse myself in the study of the words, and thoughts, and speeches, which I have carefully set down in my note-book. In brief, learning a part is the worry of my life!

XVII

MISS FORTESCUE

MISS FORTESCUE has had a career of remarkable good fortune. As has been said so often, on the stage opportunity is the main thing. But it is not everything. Miss Fortescue, like most of us in every walk of life, had her opportunity, earlier perhaps than the average, but she had also the wit and the ability for turning it to the best advantage. Endowed with much grace of personality, a full melodious voice, and that capacity for taking pains which has been said to amount to genius itself, Miss Fortescue also possesses the rarest gift of all—genuine emotional power. Her first appearance on the stage took place at the Opera Comique in 1881, when she gave a very pleasing performance of Lady Ella in "Patience." Leaving comic opera in 1884, the young actress went to the Court Theatre, under Messrs. Cecil and Clayton's management, and there she played Dorothy, the only female character in Mr. Gilbert's fine play, "Dan'l Druce." In 1885, after appearing at the Strand in the first revival of "Our Boys," she embarked upon her first tour as Galatea, and in the autumn of that year added to her repertoire the heroine of "Frou-Frou," and Lady Challoner in "Maud's Peril."

In 1886 she first essayed Vere Herbert in Mr. Hamilton's adaptation of "Moths," which has become one of her most popular impersonations; and in the autumn of the same year Miss Fortescue went out to America, playing with great success in all the principal cities of the States. She returned to the English stage in 1887, and has since then been touring with unfailing success. Miss Fortescue is an established provincial favourite, and her excellently-selected and ably-conducted company is one of those repertoire companies—all too few—that are doing a great service to the stage in maintaining the standard of the higher drama in the country. Miss Fortescue has made occasional appearances in London during the last ten years, although her energies have mainly been directed to building up her provincial enterprise, and in 1895 she undertook a most successful tour in South Africa, which promises to be as fine a field for English actors some day as America is at present. To her accomplishments as an actress she adds those of a brilliant conversationalist, and is quite as charming off as on the stage.

Miss Fortescue's opinions will be found very clearly stated in the subjoined contribution:—

I suppose I must include myself with those who do not think that acting is entirely an art, inasmuch as it is so largely a question of one's individuality. The body of an actor or an actress enters so vitally into the acting that it tends to diminish what is essentially art in acting. The lack of a striking personality interferes vitally with the success of an actor, who, given this absent personality, might be regarded as a great actor. He might not be more of an artist, however, and hence, it is evident that acting is not purely an art, as art should not rely for effect on personality. Acting, then, seems to me to be the conveying of one's conception of character or passion to others by means of one's personality. Of the qualities that attract most it is quite impossible to say; for what may please one person will repel another; and it is the actor or actress who attracts most people by the force, by the magnetism, of his or her personality who becomes the popular, the successful, if not the greatest actor or actress—"the drama's laws, the drama's patrons give."

Broadly speaking, I would say that "style" is the touchstone of acting; and by "style" I mean the manner in which the actor has developed the capacity for reproducing nature, the capacity for clothing thought in its proper garb. Many actors can suggest a thought, an idea, a passion; many can show you the outer raiment of these; but those who can present you with both are they who are the greatest among actors. I would give all for that! As to how one can best acquire this style, I am sure I do not know. There are no set laws in acting. Nor do I believe are there set methods of study. Many men, many minds. I don't think I could even describe my own methods of study; I am not sure that I have any! I study no two characters under the same conditions; but I go steadily on the lines that if you can but think the thing you will do it; so that my first concern is to get "in touch" with the character I am to represent on the stage.

Of course, as acting is largely the reproduction of the manners of different times, it is necessary that the actor or actress should study the history of the time in which the character that he or she is to impersonate is placed, and endeavour, to the best of his or her ability, to realise the manners and customs of that time as they bear upon the part. In the case of a part in a modern play, there is the life around us to be noted and studied by the actor. I might also add that the actor and actress should possess a sound mind in a sound body; for it is obvious that the healthiest and most beautiful art must come out of the healthiest and most beautiful body and soul.

Only in a slight degree do I think an actress can "feel" her parts. How could an actress, night after night, *feel* the acute joys and sorrows of such characters as Volumnia, Constance, or Juliet, without being physically affected and having her health impaired? You should not "feel" them, but you should be able to understand and sympathise with them, else you could not truthfully represent them.

As for the stage as a career, I think the only way is for each to work out his, or her, own salvation. It is a hard battle for position, and many must go down in the fight. Yet, I am not quite sure it would be better were it otherwise. That is a cruel law, perhaps; but look at nature, it is the same all over. And nature, like Hamlet, "must be cruel only to be kind."

G. Fortescue

XVIII

MR. ARTHUR BOURCHIER

FEW young actors have such opportunities for gaining experience while still amateurs as fell to the lot of Mr. Arthur Bourchier. He had always had a keen taste for theatricals, and this was whetted considerably by private performances at Eton; and soon after he went up to Christ's College the authorities at Oxford, who had hitherto looked upon the performances of play-acting undergrads with disfavour, took up a more gracious attitude, and the now famous O.U.D.C. was formed, with Canon Scott Holland, the Rev. and Hon. J. G. Adderley, Mr. W. L. Courtney, and Mr. Bourchier among its most active members. Before going to Oxford, Mr. Bourchier had played Shylock, Hotspur, Julius Cæsar, Falstaff in "The Merry Wives of Windsor," the Clown in "Twelfth Night," and Sir John Vesey in "Money." It is not surprising, therefore, that Mr. Bourchier should be a firm believer in amateur acting as training for a professional career.

He had no intention of going on the stage when he took his degree and left the university. He was reading for the bar, when one day an offer came from Mrs. Langtry of an engagement with her provincial company, and it was under the auspices of that lady that he made his first professional appearance in 1889, playing Jaques in "As You Like It." The spring of the succeeding year found him in London, and when Mrs. Langtry's season at the St. James's was closed, he boldly ventured into management on his own account, taking that theatre for a short time. Joining the Criterion company in the autumn—after further experience in the provinces with Miss Fortescue—he played Charles Courtley in "London Assurance," and Joseph in "School for Scandal." Not long afterwards, when in America with Mr. Daly, he was cast for Charles in the same piece. He subsequently played with Mr. Daly in London, was Robin Hood in Lord Tennyson's play, then the hero of "The Derby Winner," and afterwards appeared in several characters with Mr. Hare at the Garrick. He is now permanently on the roll of our actor-managers, his recent tenancy of the Royalty Theatre having been eminently successful.

Mr. Bourchier writes me to this effect :—

As regards the method I find best for studying a part, I think the best way is to first of all read the part through, and get thoroughly identified with all its points. Imagine yourself to be the character you are to represent, losing your own identity entirely. After reading the part I would advise writing the same out and getting "word perfect." Always play the part the same; never think that when you have performed it for some time you can afford to be indifferent. I believe in playing a part exactly the same every night.

As regards beginners, I would strongly advise any young person who wishes to become an actor, or actress, as the case may be, to enlist for a season under the management of Miss Sarah Thorne, for instance, as I feel sure that if a person has any ability at all it is sure to assert itself under such auspices. My advice to young actors is—"Act what you can—Where you can—and, above all—WHEN you can."

Arthur Bourchier

XIX

MR. H. REEVES-SMITH

MR. H. REEVES-SMITH is an earnest, conscientious actor, of excellent presence, clever in light comedy, and sympathetic in more tender assumptions. His experience of the stage has been long and varied. Born at Scarborough—where his father, Mr. G. Reeves-Smith, was then manager of the Spa, being latterly manager of the Brighton Aquarium—he was educated at Edmonstone House, Worthing, and had just left school when, in 1878, he made his first appearance on the stage. The event took place at Halifax, in Miss Heath's production of "Jane Shore," and the young actor appeared under the *sobriquet* of "H. R. Shafton." After a few weeks' tour with "Jane Shore," Mr. Reeves-Smith was lucky enough to join Mr. Wilson Barrett at the Theatre Royal, Hull, in one of the last of the fast disappearing stock-companies, and during two seasons there he gained much valuable experience in the practice of his art. His period of provincial probation was destined to be much shorter than was then the rule, as he proceeded direct from Hull to London and made his metropolitan début at the old Olympic as Richard Hare in "East Lynne," when he dropped his *nom-de-théâtre*, and appeared as H. Reeves-Smith. October 17, 1879, saw him "creating" Tom Lilford in H. J. Byron's "Courtship," at the old Court Theatre, and after the run of that piece he played Dolly in "Betsy" for seventeen months in the provinces—a sharp change from his experience in the Hull stock-company.

A six months' visit to America in the winter of 1881–82, as a member of Mr. Abbey's Park Theatre company, followed, and on 22nd April 1882 we find him back in London again, playing in "Long Ago," at the Royalty. He next joined Miss Davenport's company at Toole's Theatre, and afterwards appeared in a revival of the sprightly "Betsy," at the Criterion, a tour with the Vokes family, and an engagement with Mr. J. Clarke at the Strand, following in quick succession. He was then engaged by Mr. Charles Hawtrey to play Harry Marsland in "The Private Secretary," at the Prince's, in March 1884, and subsequently filled the same part for several months at the Globe. For over a hundred nights Mr. Reeves-Smith appeared as Charles Middlewick with the late David James in "Our Boys," at the Strand, returning to the Globe again. In 1885 he was at the old Court Theatre once more, impersonating Bertie Fitzurse in "New Men and Old Acres," Herbert in "Young Mrs. Winthrop," and other characters, and fifteen months later joined Messrs. Hare and Kendal at the St. James's to play Andrew Moorcraft in "Money." In London, "on tour," and in America, Mr. Reeves-Smith has since appeared in scores of characters, such as Dick Dowlas, Felix Featherley, Joseph Surface, Beauseant, Sir Lucius O'Trigger, Dudley Smooth, Clement Hale, and Lord Maidment, only to mention a few that readily occur to the memory; his name is seldom out of the play-bill of one or other of the principal theatres; he is, in short, an excellent, all round, reliable actor.

Mr. Reeves-Smith writes me as follows:—

The first thing a would-be actor has to consider is the question of suitability for the calling which he contemplates adopting. This is absolutely imperative; but it is a consideration which many ignore, with the frequent result that from the first they are foredoomed to failure. Having satisfied one's self that one possesses the aptitude for the work, and taking it for granted that such a one is sincerely desirous of striving to do his very best in any part, be that important or unimportant, it is necessary to recognise some well-defined method of study, and on this point I may say that my experience has served to show me that the best way to study a part is to read, in the first place, the whole of the play, and to thoroughly understand its purpose and meaning—though this at times may be found a matter of some difficulty.

After having done this, then turn your attention to the words. Get these into your head, attend plenty of rehearsals, and do not mumble at these, but try and act. Finally, the part must be played in the "make-up" clothes and properties which will be used on its production before the public. In my opinion this should be done at least twice before the public representation. In following out this system ease is secured in mind and in body—nothing is left to chance. If failure be the result, there is at least the satisfaction of knowing that you have done your best to secure success. Work, practice, and experience alone can produce a finished actor. Without them a temporary position may be attained by a part being particularly suited to certain peculiarities of the actor, but it cannot be maintained, and the consequence is, that the career of one who so obtains a momentary success resembles the proverbial rocket and the stick.

H. Nevil Smith

XX

MR. BASSETT ROE

It would have been strange if one who had served his apprenticeship in the provinces under such sterling actors as Barry Sullivan and William Creswick, and possessed all the attributes which we look for in a good actor—voice, physique, "personality"—had not succeeded in making his mark on the London stage. But Mr. Bassett Roe had only a comparatively short career in the Metropolis when he could lay claim to an established reputation; indeed, he has for several years been a leading London actor, although his metropolitan experience has just encompassed one decade.

It was at the Princess's Theatre, in July 1887, that he made his first bow to a London audience, as the Detective in "The Shadows of a Great City." In the plays which succeeded that at the same theatre he was entrusted with the representation of prominent parts; and in November of 1888 he was at the Shaftesbury, under the management of Mrs. Lancaster Wallis, playing with great success Beauséant in the "Lady of Lyons." Back again at the Princess's in the summer of the succeeding year, he was there cast for the rôle of Sir Ralph Minto in "True Heart," a part which he "created" to the entire satisfaction of criticdom.

Mr. Roe next transferred his services to the Adelphi,

where, as King Lycas in Mr. Robert Buchanan's play, "The Bride of Love," but especially as Sir Philip Kingston in "The English Rose," he was eminently successful, playing the latter part during the nine months' run of the piece. In the summer of 1891 he was at the Avenue, playing with the greatest effect Watson Flint, the unemotional stockbroker in Mr. Bronson Howard's clever, but not very successful comedy, "The Henrietta"; and, again, we find him back once more at the Princess's in "Fate and Fortune," and "Arrah-na-Pogue"; then at the Vaudeville, where he impersonated Mad Antony in Mr. Joseph Hatton's version of "Prince and Pauper." A season at the New Olympic followed, and here Mr. Roe appeared as Prince Talleyrand in "A Royal Divorce," the Emperor Justinian in "Theodora," and Bill Syke in "Oliver Twist," the last-named impersonation placing the seal upon his rapidly-earned reputation. Thus, in the course of a very few years from his first appearance in London, he had succeeded in firmly establishing himself as an actor possessed of quick intelligence, and a high degree of histrionic power. To indicate his versatility it is only necessary to say that among numerous other characters which he has impersonated from time to time may be mentioned Joseph Surface, Jaques ("As You Like It"), Mercutio, Marat ("Ninon"), Prince Zouroff ("Moths"), Rolando ("The Honeymoon"), Henri Vaudelle ("Esther Sandraz"), Nathan the Apostate ("Leah"), Hubert ("King John"), &c. &c.

Mr. Bassett Roe has some very practical advice to offer to "the beginner on the stage" in the following letter which he has addressed to me:—

It is a common mistake of beginners, as soon as their parts are given them, to learn the words by rote—cues and all. Not having the context, they are quite at sea as to the meaning of their lines, and inevitably give wrong inflections to the simplest sentences. It is always best to attend at least one or two rehearsals before committing any of the words to memory. Let them get a general idea of the entire piece, and especially of those scenes in which they are chiefly concerned. Then find out what relation their parts bear to the general scheme, and after having thought out the stage business, the characterisation, and the positions allotted them by the stage manager, the mere words will come readily enough of themselves. The reversal of this procedure counts for much of the mechanical, lifeless acting in minor parts.

In studying classical rôles, imagination and poetic insight are chiefly essential; whereas in "creating" modern ones, observation is, perhaps, of more service, together with a happy knack of reproducing mannerisms, tones, and idiosyncrasies to be met with in the life around us. The chief difficulty experienced by the actor nowadays is the lack of opportunity of doing effective work. "Give me the opportunity," he cries, "and all will be well." Hence the somewhat cynical saying, "The Art of Acting is the art of getting good parts."

Bassett Roe

XXI

MISS KATE PHILLIPS

THIS delightful actress affords one of those instances wherein the necessity of earning a living has induced gifted men and women to turn to the stage—very much to the stage's advantage. The daughter of a well-known fox-hunting squire, the late Mr. Philip Goldney, of Broadleigh Hall, Essex, Miss Phillips, at a crisis in the fortunes of her family, found that she would have to earn her bread and butter before eating it, and with a quiet heroism, which has since been well rewarded, the charming young lady faced the inevitable by engaging as a nursery governess. While so employed she happened to take part in some amateur theatricals, and finding that she could bear a part with more than tolerable grace, she lost no time in deciding to make the most of her new-found talent. Her first professional appearance was made as a page in "Chilperic" at the Lyceum, and then the young actress went on a provincial tour, from which she returned to London to score many successes at the Prince of Wales's, the Court, the St. James's, and the Vaudeville Theatres, remaining at the last-named for four seasons.

In illustration of the versatility of this brilliant and sparkling actress one need only mention her performances of Gerda in "The White Pilgrim," Maria in "Twelfth Night," Phœbe in "Paul Pry," Lady Franklin in "Money," Dot in "The Cricket on the Hearth," Mrs. Pomfret in "The Paper Chase," Cerisette in "The Dead Heart," Lady Gay Spanker in "London Assurance," Susan in "Nance Oldfield," Nerissa in "The Merchant of Venice," Margery in "Becket," &c.

In 1890 Miss Phillips entered into an engagement with the manager of the Lyceum, and was a member of Sir Henry's company for several seasons. She has latterly been further proving her versatility by achieving success in a musical piece. She is an established favourite, and her name is seldom out of the London play-bills.

Miss Kate Phillips's opinions are stated very concisely in the appended extracts from a letter which I have received from her:—

I consider that the best methods of study for aspirants are, first, to "walk on" at one of our leading theatres in London—say, the Lyceum, Haymarket, Criterion, or St. James's—where they would have all the advantages of good stage management, besides seeing and being associated with the best acting of the day. To remain, say, a season, and then to move on to another theatre, where one could see different styles and methods. For a time a line or two might fall to the lot of the student, and so on to better parts.

Both men and women should study fencing and dancing; and, of course, a thorough knowledge of Shakespeare's plays is a liberal education. I would advise, as a first lesson, Hamlet's advice to the players—that, at all times, should be laid thoroughly to heart. To a young actor or actress I should say, "Move about; don't remain too long in the one place."

Kate Phillips

XXII

MR. LEONARD OUTRAM

Mr. Leonard Outram has had a career of great activity and considerable distinction. He was not a child of the stage, his parents having no connection with the profession. Born on the 9th April 1855, he was educated at Dulwich, but early manifesting a hankering for the footlights he placed himself, when a young man, under the tuition of Thomas Coe, then stage manager of the Haymarket Theatre, and made his first professional appearance in the summer of 1876. He joined the Shakespearian company of Mr. and Mrs. Daniel E. Bandmann, and first played Rosencrantz in "Hamlet." In 1879 he went out to America, and had five years' theatrical experience there, supporting the Italian tragedian, Salvini, and other "stars." He was back on the English stage again in 1884, and managed the Torquay Theatre during 1886–87. In 1890 he revived Wills's "Juanna" in London, writing and producing about this period several plays, among which may be mentioned "A Mighty Error," "The Fiat of the Gods," and "April Rain." He was manager of the Avenue Theatre in 1891, and of the Globe Theatre the following year. He revisited America with Mr. Beerbohm Tree in 1894, and during the 1895–96 season he was managing the Olympic, where he produced, with considerable success, the drama "True Blue," of which he was part author, and which represented the first attempt to deal on the stage in a realistic way with the Royal Navy. He has gone back to America with Mr. Beerbohm Tree, on the visit which that manager has undertaken as these lines are being written.

In the course of a letter to me on the subject of stage study, Mr. Outram writes:—

My methods of study as an actor have been, first, to acquaint myself with the meaning of the play and the bearing of my own part upon its story and situations. I then analyse the character I am to play, and aim at rendering every passage consistently.

I next seek to emphasise the effects of the part and to colour it vividly, and I avail myself of all the assistance which "business," limelight, incidental music, &c. &c., can give. Reciprocity with those I am playing with I regard as most important—I mean that each actor should feed and score off his companions in the scene. My plan is to first satisfy the *ear*, then the eye, and finally the intellect of one's audience. To be clearly heard is vital; to look what one represents is essential; to convey the author's meaning is indispensable.

Leonard Outram

XXIII

MR. ERIC LEWIS

Mr. Eric Lewis is one of those accomplished entertainers who have conquered two theatrical worlds. He has proved himself equally at home in Comic Opera and in Comedy, and has always been distinguished for that high degree of refinement with which he invests even his most comical creations. Mr. Lewis is the polished gentleman to his finger tips, and seems to have been destined by Nature to portray the witty, frivolous nobleman, who is one of the most enduring of theatrical "types." But in saying this, it must not be presumed that his range of character is by any means circumscribed, as a glance at the long and varied list of parts in which he has appeared from time to time with complete success affords abundant proof of his versatility as an actor. His humour is at once genial and quaint, and, in this respect, he may be said to bear a certain affinity to Mr. George Grossmith; though, curiously enough, he commenced his career in the character in which that most delightful comedian has elected to appear in his later days. That is to say, Mr. Lewis made his first bow to the public as a purveyor of that form of entertainment known as "the musical sketch," his initial appearance taking place, in October 1879, at St. James's Hall, Brighton, in conjunction with Mr. and Mrs. Arthur Law.

His London début was made at the Royal Polytechnic during the Christmas season of 1880–81, and there he gave his musical sketches until the "Poly" ceased to be a place of amusement, having, meanwhile, been a frequent substitute for the late Corney Grain at the St. George's Hall. Towards the close of 1881 we find Mr. Lewis playing Lord Glenmuir in Maurice Barrymore's adaptation, "Honour," and for the greater part of the succeeding year he was on tour with Mdme. Alice Barth's Opera Company, playing a round of characters. In November of the same year he joined the Savoy Company, remaining a member until 1887, when he turned his attention to the more essentially dramatic work, and has since appeared in London and the provinces in numerous comedy parts, though one of his most notable subsequent successes was obtained by his delightful impersonation of the Duke of Fayensberg in "La Cigale," which was produced at the Lyric on 9th October 1890, his splendid performance being in no small degree responsible for the great success which attended that production.

Mr. Lewis's methods of study are clearly and concisely stated in the following letter which I have received from him:—

In reply to your polite inquiries as to my method of studying a part, I usually try the following, viz.: As soon as I get the part I copy it into a penny memorandum book, and after the first rehearsal, when I mark all positions, I learn it as quickly as I can, so as to be able to rehearse without a book. This gives me a chance of feeling easy with my arms, and allows me to do "business," which is impossible if you have to hold a book all the time. Also as soon as I know my "words," I never go out without repeating them—sometimes to the amusement of passers-by; and I find an excellent plan is to always go through the part the last thing at night, as it comes so wonderfully fresh in the morning.

This also applies to musical parts, as I find that when I once get the notes and words in my head, it gives me all the more time to devote to "light and shade," positions, and—which I think important—appearing at ease. In the course of sixteen years' experience, I find nothing so difficult as "repose on the stage." If I might offer a word of advice to beginners, it would be, *Always act* at rehearsal; never trust that "It'll be all right at night," &c. &c. Ten to one it won't.

Eric Lewis.

XXIV

MR. ARTHUR PLAYFAIR

This clever comedian first came into prominence as an exceptionally-gifted mimic; but before his engagement at the Princes' Hall, where he reproduced, for the delectation of admiring audiences, the idiosyncracies of the principal London actors and music-hall artistes, he had gone through a varied apprenticeship on the regular stage. His first part was the small one of Mr. Chapstone in "Jim the Penman," but the more important part of Captain Redwood in the same play was afterwards assigned to him while under Mr. Balsir Chatterton's management. In 1888 Mrs. Bernard Beere engaged him to play Burdock in her production of "Masks and Faces," at the Opera Comique; and at the close of the London season he went on tour with Mr. Charles Terry's company, playing Cecil in "Barbara" and Edward Fairlegh in "Hook and Eye." He then accepted an engagement with Mr. and Mrs. Kendal in Manchester for a season, and was subsequently engaged by Mr. Beerbohm Tree to fill the parts of Marshall in "Captain Swift" and the Judge in "A Man's Shadow." He next played Sir Toby, at the Criterion, in the revival of "School for Scandal" during 1891, and afterwards came out as a mimic, being engaged by Mr. Horace Sedger to burlesque Mr. Tree in "The

Prancing Girl" at the Prince of Wales's, and then to create the part of Giorgio in "The Mountebanks," at the Lyric.

More recently Mr. Playfair has gone in for musical comedy, of which his rich flexible voice, his mobile features, and his unctuous humour, all serve to make him a most successful exponent. He has played several of the "Arthur Roberts' parts" with all the fun of that excellent mime, and with—shall I say?—rather more refinement. Mr. Playfair comes of a very distinguished family, being the grandson of Colonel Sir Hugh Lyon Playfair, who was Provost of St. Andrews—which is now mainly celebrated as the home of that genial chatterbox, "A. K. H. B."—and the youngest son of Major-General A. L. Playfair, of H.M. Indian Army. His cousin is Lord Playfair, who has a brilliant Parliamentary record. Born in India in 1869, he was educated at St. Mary's College, Oscott, near Birmingham, where he early showed proclivities for theatricals. It was intended that, like so many of his distinguished family, he should join the service; but after a year spent at the Oxford Military College, he decided for the sock and buskin and against the boot and saddle. The army lost thereby a very handsome officer, and the stage gained a gentleman with a delightful humorous gift and the capacity for giving that natural and artistic expression.

Mr. Playfair, in the course of an amusing letter, writes me as follows:—

Personally I never can learn any part "like a parrot," but after I have all my business "pat" at rehearsal my "words" always come into my head quite naturally. If I had a little brother who *wanted* to be an actor, I would try to get him into such a combination as the "Compton Comedy Company"; for I am absolutely convinced that to play a new part every few nights is the *only* way to gain experience.

Fencing is, without any two opinions, the very best method to acquire an easy and graceful bearing, and this should be one of the most important considerations with any one who desires to make the best of the actor's art. I always advise every single soul I know to try every other profession before the stage; for, *unless* a person is willing to *work*, *work*, *work*, and plod on, and "rough it," he may be sure he will never, never succeed as any true artist should.

Mr. Playfair being one of the cleverest mimics of the time, his views on mimicry are of especial interest. In this connection he says:—

Although I am open to correction on the point, it is my firm belief that in nine cases out of ten, the gift of mimicry is not an acquired but a hereditary one. At all events, it unquestionably is so in my own case. My grandfather possessed the accomplishment in an eminent degree, and some of his talents descended on me through my father, who likewise excels as a mimic, though his abilities in this respect have never been witnessed by the public.

The first attempt made by me was during my school-days, when I succeeded in affording some little amusement to my fellow-students in "taking off" the different masters, although that little amusement resulted, more than once, in serious trouble to myself!

Theatrical performances have invariably been the source of the most intense pleasure to me; and after having witnessed, for the first time, the performance of some leading London actor, many is the hour I used to spend in front of my large mirror for the purpose of catching his facial expressions and movements. When I have once seen an actor on the stage, I never experience any difficulty in deciding whether my efforts to impersonate him are likely to prove successful.

Arthur Playfair

XXV

MR. JAMES WELCH

MR. JAMES WELCH is an actor of whom the dramatic world is pretty sure to hear a good deal more in the future. Those who have watched his career with interest know that as a character actor there are few at present on the stage to equal him. Mr. Welch began life as an accountant in Liverpool, but amateur theatricals lured him to the regular footlights, which he first faced in earnest under the auspices of Mr. Wilson Barrett. Since then he has been slowly but surely climbing up the ladder of fame, the greatest difficulty he has had to overcome being his own innate modesty. In the autumn of 1896 he made his first essay in management, and had a most successful six weeks' season at Terry's, where he staged "My Artful Valet." He has since been a leading member of Mr. Wyndham's company at the Criterion. He and Mr. Richard Le Gallienne were youthful friends, and three years ago Mr. Welch married the poet's sister.

Mr. Welch has something of interest to say concerning the beginner on the stage in the following contribution :—

Beginners must learn that success on the stage does not depend entirely upon natural ability. Hazlitt said that success depended on "accident, opportunity, and encouragement." Nowadays, I should say, it depends—

30 per cent. on ability, 10 per cent. on training, 30 per cent. on opportunity or chance, and 30 per cent. on business capacity; indeed, so important is this latter quality, that without it a beginner may have any amount of ability, he may get training, and even opportunity, and still not get on. Training and one's own power of artistic selection will do this; but to get fully recognised by the outside world, to be a successful actor, one must know how best to push and how best to work one's self. After all, I suppose a tradesman with the finest article in the world to sell must still advertise it.

A great variety of points are to be considered by those who wish to go on the stage. Am I fitted mentally and bodily? Have I got the necessary temperament, the mimetic quality? Have I got the spirit and heart to bear up under countless heartbreaking disappointments? Have I got sufficient will force or that wholesome determined obstinacy which is even better than will in the face of obstacles? And above all, the art must be taken up honestly and seriously. The stage and the Church have been too long thought the dust-heaps for family failures. The beginner must be prepared to work hard, and often under that most difficult of conditions, with no immediate goal in view.

He must also remember that the stage is an epitome (as Hazlitt said), a bettered likeness of the world, with the dull part left out. Tragedy is an imitation of life in passions; it is comedy only which imitates both passions and habits. And in representing the former the beginner must learn to subordinate impulse to law. "In the very torrent, tempest, and, as I may say, whirlwind of passion, you must acquire and beget a temperance that may give it smoothness." "Be not too tame, neither," Shakespeare quickly adds, lest his advice should be misunderstood, "but let your own discretion be your tutor." Yes, the beginner's discretion must tell him when he has hit upon the right tone and right expression, which must first be suggested to him by his own feelings. In endeavouring to express emotions he will try various tones, various gestures, various accelerations and retardations of the rhythm; and during this tentative process his vigilant discretion will arrest those that are effective and discard the rest.

Having something like an intellectual appreciation of the sequences of feeling and their modes of manifestation, the actor has next to select out of these such as his own physical qualifications enable him to reproduce effectively, and such as will be universally intelligible. Hence, the actor is forced to be as typical as the poet or any other artist is. No artist pretends closely to copy nature, but only to represent nature sublimated into the ideal. The nearer we approach to every-day reality implied by the author in his characters and language, the closer the coat-and-waistcoat realism of the drama, the closer must be the actor's imitation of every-day manners; but even then he must idealise, *i.e.* select and heighten, and it is for his tact to determine how much.

One more word to the beginner. Let him remember that complete selective realism on the stage is most certainly to be aimed at. Remember, too, that realism on the stage does not only consist of real water, real railway trains, real steam-rollers and mud-dredgers. To have realism in perfection we must have real actors; and, above all, let us be modest, consider ourselves beginners always, and take care not too recklessly to cheapen the sacred secret of the mysterious world behind the scenes.

James Welch

PART IV

TWO "SCHOOLS" FOR ACTING

TWO "SCHOOLS" FOR ACTING

THERE are many points on which the contributors to this work are at variance; but there is one upon which they are all agreed — the advantage of varied work. Nearly every one laments the disappearance of the old stock-companies and their substitution by the modern system of "long runs" and touring companies. But, happily, there are still in existence a number of dramatic combinations, which, while neither London touring companies, carrying the latest sensation and so many tons of scenery, nor stock-companies in the old sense of the term, represent what may be described as the happy mean between these two, and are, perhaps, superior in some respects to both. I refer to the "repertoire" companies, of which I might name those of Mr. Edward Compton, Mr. Osmond Tearle, Mr. F. R. Benson, Mr. Edmund Tearle, Mr. Louis Calvert, Mr. Ben Greet, and several others. If one could say with confidence that there was a tendency towards the increase of such companies as these, then one might cease to regret the disappearance of the old stock system. For, so far as these companies are concerned, they represented what is even an improvement on the old stock-companies; they provide a wide and varied range of work for the young actor, while affording him sufficient time to study his part before appearing in it, and they supply him with a constant change of audience. The advantage of all these to the young actor need not be dwelt upon; and when we consider how much better staged, how much better "dressed" they are, and how much more care is bestowed in every respect upon the productions of a good repertoire company than was thought necessary in the old "stock" days, we are forced to the conclusion that, so far as the repertoire system exists, it represents a distinct advance in the theatric art. Take any of Mr. Compton's productions, most of Mr. Osmond Tearle's, of Mr. Benson's—his "Julius Cæsar," his "Midsummer Night's Dream," for examples—or Mr. Louis Calvert's admirable revival of "Henry IV.," any of these is worthy of a London audience—and that could not be said to be the case with "stock" productions fifteen or twenty years ago.

But, unfortunately, there are few signs just now to lead us to hope for the multiplication of such companies as these. The "scratch teams" of mimics sent into the country by speculative London managers with "the latest London success"—which, in nine cases out of ten, would be more truthfully described as the latest London failure—comprise at the present time the staple fare of the provincial playgoer. But the provincial playgoer is as intelligent a human being as his London compeer, and he is rebelling against this treatment, as is evidenced by the fact that not one of the numerous London failures that have been foisted upon the provinces within recent years has met with any measure of success. One is inclined, therefore, to think that "things will take a turn," and it may not be too much to hope that the near future will see a wholesome movement in the direction of new repertoire companies which, in the opinion of those best qualified to speak on this subject, afford the finest nursing ground for dramatic talent. In this connection it has occurred to me that a portion of the present work might not unfitly be devoted to the views and opinions of two of the best-known conductors of repertoire companies—Mr. Edward Compton and Mr. Osmond Tearle.

I—COMEDY

MR. EDWARD COMPTON

THERE is no name more honoured in the stage history of the present century than that of Henry Compton, nor is there a better instance of a son inheriting an honoured name, and maintaining it with dignity and respect, than the way in which Mr. Edward Compton has worn the stage name of his father. Mr. Edward Compton comes of excellent intellectual stock. His father, whose private name was Charles Mackenzie, himself a man of great ability and one of the most accomplished comedians who have ever trod the stage, was the brother of Dr. Mackenzie, a celebrated physician in his day, whose son was the still more celebrated Sir Morell Mackenzie; while the Rev. Morell Mackenzie was another brother, who reached eminence as the occupant of the Presidential Chair of Biblical Criticism and Church History at the Glasgow Independent Academy, and whose death, in 1843, on board the ill-fated steamer *Pegasus*, which foundered off Holy Island, and went down with forty-four of the fifty passengers on board, was heroic in the highest degree. Here, it will be readily admitted, is unmistakable evidence of an excellent stock, and if Dr. Mackenzie's fame as a physician was even outshone by the subsequent celebrity of his distinguished son, the fame which

Mr. Charles Mackenzie won for his stage name of Compton has not diminished in the keeping of his gifted son Edward.

It was even more certain that the son of Henry Compton would become an actor than that the son of Dr. Mackenzie would become a physician; for, contrive as actors may to place their children in other professions, there is a fatal fascination about the actor's calling which is irresistible to sons and daughters of the stage, and though they may for a time follow some other profession, they generally gravitate towards the footlights sooner or later, and sue for fame, fortune, or a "living wage," where their father or mother, or both, have fought for these before. Mr. Edward Compton had four years "in the City" before definitely turning to the stage, and this business training has since stood him in good stead as the proprietor and manager of the Compton Comedy Company. His early stage career presents no remarkable features, other than that he had gained an excellent all-round experience before he was twenty-five years of age, having been the "leading man" in stock-companies at Glasgow, Birmingham, Liverpool, Bristol, and other important towns, a fact that is sufficient to indicate how hard and arduous was his work in his early days. He is best known to the public in connection with his admirable Comedy Company, during the long and brilliant career of which he has produced so many gems of old English comedy, and appeared with so much acceptance in a score or so of famous character parts, among which his admirable Davy Garrick, his Charles Surface, his Goldfinch, and his Tony Lumpkin are, perhaps, the most popular.

Having determined to place Mr. Compton on the inquisitorial rack for the purpose of this work, I journeyed down to one of the large towns in the

Midlands, where the Compton Comedy Company was delighting the local playgoers, and searching out the celebrated comedian at his apartments, found him just at the fag-end of his daily correspondence, the manuscripts of possible and impossible plays lying about his table in picturesque disorder, together with many curious and interesting items of correspondence. Here, for instance, is how an enthusiastic admirer of the actor had opened a letter of four closely-written pages to him that very day, referring to his performance in the play scene in "Edmund Kean," when he appears as Hamlet:—"Man, god, or devil! Whatever you are, let me thank you for your Hamlet last night! I had thought, after seeing so many Hamlets, that I should *never* come across the man that would *feel* the immortal soliloquy as I feel it; one that could breathe the life into each separate word as the immortal Shakespeare must have wished it. I have seen some provincial actors descanting that soliloquy as if it were the prologue to some horrible burlesque, and yet, each word has a world of thought in it somewhere, hidden deeply it may be. Is it not the actor's province to discover these hidden thoughts? . . . On Monday I saw your Garrick and marvelled, on Tuesday your Lumpkin, and, after Garrick, was surprised. To-night you were *great*, wonderful!" That is surely an unique tribute to a comedian; but I think Mr. Compton prizes most of all the little scrap of crumpled paper, torn from a notebook or diary, and sent round to him behind the scenes on his last visit to the Gaiety Theatre, Dublin, with these simple words scribbled upon it by an enthusiastic pitite, "By jabers, you *can* act." This also referred to his impersonation of Kean.

"The story of the Compton Comedy Company is not without interest, I think, Mr. Compton?"

"Yes, it may be worthy of a few words, for the company owes its origin to what was, in some respects, an accident——"

"Like many other great things," I venture to suggest, "the discovery of the law of gravitation, for instance!"

Mr. Compton blushes modestly, and continues: "My father never had any speculation in him; he was always chary of risking his earnings in the organisation of a company, and even after he left the Haymarket and 'starred' in the provinces, he did so as a salaried actor. In this he was judicious, and it speaks well for his solicitude for his family, that, rather than strive to enrich himself and so risk his regular earnings, he preferred not to endanger his assured income, and the means whereby he provided for the wants of his domestic circle. I was in the full flush of youth then, however, and would have had him plunge into all the uncertainties of theatrical speculation. Meeting him at Liverpool, when I was in the stock-company there, I laid before him a scheme for forming a Compton Comedy Company, with him as its leading attraction and your humble servant as manager and light comedian. My father, however, was seized with his last illness soon after this, and my project came to naught. Shortly afterwards I went out to America with Miss Adelaide Neilson, with whom I played on the other side of the Atlantic for about a year, meeting with exceptional success as Malvolio in 'Twelfth Night'—a character very dissimilar to my usual line. Coming back to England again, I found myself with a modest amount of capital at my command, having been careful to husband my resources in America, and having no immediate work on hand, I said to myself, 'Now is the time to set about the formation of a company on my own account.' The old idea became a resolution, the resolution a fixed purpose, and I set to work to organise a company in which I should play the characters that had so long been associated with the name of my deceased father. I succeeded in forming the company, among whose members were Mr. Lewis Ball, who is my stage manager to this day, and Miss Virginia Bateman, who subsequently became Mrs. Compton. Our first tour turned out successful when I reckoned it up at the end; and we continued, meeting with our ups and downs—especially our downs—for a time, until the Compton Comedy Company had become an established favourite with provincial audiences. We have now been fifteen years 'on tour.'"

"How is it, Mr. Compton, that your company should have been so signally successful, while failure has been the fate of so many other comedy combinations?"

"Well, I could scarcely give an opinion on that head without being held to be invidious. But this I will say, that the steady progress which has been made by my company during the fifteen years of its existence is due, in a great measure, to the fact that I have relied on an excellent all-round company, instead of going in for one or two 'stars,' and completing the company with a scratch team. Then my early business training has been of great value to me, and I have always managed the affairs of the company on essentially business lines, being content with a modest success for a time, and so progressing to better things. Above all, I have never forgotten the truth of the old maxim, that you must 'cut your coat according to your cloth.' Disregard of these things may be held to account for the failure which, as you say, has generally attended others who have endeavoured to establish touring companies in English comedy."

"Your company has been spoken of as one of the finest 'schools' of acting in which a clever young man or woman might wish to study. There must be some potent reason for this, above the mere fact of your producing so many different plays, and I presume it admits of a simple explanation."

"I am aware that my company has come to be regarded as quite a little school, where dramatic talent is afforded an opportunity to ripen and expand. If I might venture to give an opinion in this connection, I should say that any distinction which the Compton Comedy Company has achieved in the direction you indicate, has been due to a system I have observed from the very first—that of devoting as much care to the minor as to the major parts. Personally, I take the greatest pains with even the least important member of the company, in order that he or she may be as perfect in a little part as any of the principals in a leading rôle. We are constantly rehearsing, too, and whenever I have a member of the company cast for the first time for a part in a play in which I may have appeared hundreds of times before, I rehearse with him quite as diligently as if I were also to appear in it for the first time. This implies a great deal of work for me; but then it adds to the general effect, and to the all-round improvement of my company, and in that way I am well repaid. I will give you an instance of the advantage of this thorough system. Some days ago I was unexpectedly deprived of the services of one of my principals, whose absence has necessitated an important change in the cast of every play that has been announced; yet my company has played every piece as if there had been no change whatever in the cast, and up till now no less than nine different plays have been so produced, several of the players appearing in their parts for the first time. I myself have had to play both Dromios in 'The Comedy of Errors' to accomplish this, and it has entailed a deal of extra rehearsing; but the fact that, under such circumstances, we have been able to stage every play as announced, and perform it with credit, is a testimony, I venture to think, to the efficiency of the system which I have always followed out, and which I have endeavoured to indicate to you."

"You are a strong believer, of course, in the need of varied work for young actors?"

"Certainly. There is nothing more injurious to acting than the modern system of long runs and London touring companies, consisting of young men and women who have learned their parts like parrots, from watching the originals in London. They go out into the provinces on a tour of so many months' duration, they have nothing to do but to mimic the London performers every night, no rehearsals, no elevating study, and is it any wonder that many of these young people should never come to any good? With a good repertoire company there is always a wholesome round of new work, and little time for loafing, and that is why good actors come out of such companies. The repertoire of the Compton Company has included: 'Twelfth Night,' 'As You Like It,' 'Comedy of Errors,' 'The Hypocrite,' 'School for Scandal,' 'The Rivals,' 'Wild Oats,' 'She Stoops to Conquer,' 'Heir-at-Law,' 'Road to Ruin,' 'Money,' 'Home' (by T. W. Robertson), 'Delicate Ground,' 'Much Ado about Nothing,' 'Romeo and Juliet,' 'The Poor Gentleman,' 'John Bull,' 'Davy Garrick,' 'The Honeymoon,' 'London Assurance,' 'The Lady of Lyons,' 'The American,' 'The Wonder,' 'Sydney Carton,' and 'Edmund Kean.' About a dozen of these excellent pieces are staged by us in the course of each annual tour, which lasts for forty-five weeks out of the fifty-two; so that the members of the company have a splendid variety of work in some of the best compositions which English dramatic literature can boast."

"I need scarcely ask whether you have many applications for admission to your company."

"Scores! Scarcely a morning passes but my correspondence includes letters from would-be actors and actresses."

"And how often do you engage beginners, may I ask?"

"I generally take a lady and gentleman each year, who have never had any stage experience before, and initiate them into the work. There are frequent changes, of course, in the lower ranks of the company, for my principals remain with me for years; and when a young actor has completed his probationary period, and finds there is no immediate chance of his getting any higher in the company, he naturally looks for fresh fields. But you will see from what I say how little room there is for beginners even in a company like my own, compared, at all events, with the numbers who are anxious to go on the stage. And I might mention here that a great many people have an idea that the first requisite of an actor is a good memory. People come to me frequently and say, 'Oh, will you hear our Johnnie, or our Lottie as the case may be, recite so-and-so (naming some piece of dreadful doggerel); he (or she) knows half-a-dozen pages right off by heart.' These good people are totally ignorant of the real essentials of an actor; for, while a good memory is useful, it is by no means the first consideration. No actor of experience ever gives much thought to mere words; if he studies his part correctly and gets into the spirit of the piece, the words will come without any great mental effort on his part."

This leads Mr. Compton on to speak of his own work. "When I am studying a new part," he says, "I ransack every obtainable book which may be calculated to assist me in arriving at a proper estimate of the character. There's my latest original piece, 'Edmund Kean,' for instance. In studying for that part I read every life of the famous tragedian that has been published, making copious notes of his most prominent characteristics as described therein, so that while I should idealise the character, I would do so on a basis of truth. Then I inspected as many pictures and engravings of Kean as I could find, in order to 'dress' the part as accurately as possible, and I had a wig made precisely the same as Kean's own hair, from the well-known engraving of the 'great little man.' I believe in being thorough in every detail, and paying as much attention to small things as to great, for you will generally find that it is in the small things that character is most strongly marked. But apart from that, it seems to me that the conscientious artist will not scamp any part of his work, no matter how unimportant it may be. Speaking for myself, I devote as much proportionate care and thought to the perfecting of a short 'curtain raiser,' or front piece, as I do to the piece of the evening; though it is doubtful if one gets full credit for this, as there is a stupid idea prevalent that the front pieces are merely intended to while away the time until the audience has assembled for the main item of the programme. But after all is said and done, though the great material reward of the actor is the approval of the public—*that* is the *sine quâ non* of success, and that we must all strive to win—there is a sense of solid satisfaction to be gained by doing one's level best from an artistic point of view, no matter what the verdict of an audience may be. And, in the generality of cases, I am convinced true art meets with the approval of a good, sensible audience.

"To the young actor my advice is, 'Neglect no opportunity of gaining a knowledge and insight into character and the human heart; study the people you meet, note their characteristics, and always strive to invest whatever part you have to play with an atmosphere of truth and reality.' Every audience is quick to recognise truthfulness to nature, and to thank the actor who presents them with it."

Edward Compton

II—TRAGEDY

MR. OSMOND TEARLE

Mr. Osmond Tearle has been styled "the Irving of the provinces." The title is well earned, and yet we could conceive no greater contrast than that between the two actors—Irving "sicklied o'er with the pale cast of thought," Tearle of robust appearance and herculean proportions. But Mr. Tearle has done for the Shakespearian drama in the provinces a similar service to that which Sir Henry has performed in London. He has devoted the better part of his life to the stage presentment of the master's noblest creations; he has demonstrated that, in the hands of a judicious manager and capable actor, Shakespeare does not "spell ruin." And in these days, when theatrical jobbers, battening on the least worthy instincts of the people, are mainly engaged in "syndicating" those ineffable monstrosities, known variously as "musical comedy-drama," and "go-as-you-please operatic, farcical burlesque," the actor who holds aloft the banner of Shakespeare and recognises none but the "legitimate" drama, is a benefactor of his species. He deserves the unstinted praise of the admirers of Shakespeare—and their name is legion—and all who believe that the mission of the stage is something nobler than the mere diversion of the thoughtless and the vulgar. In this respect, then,

Mr. Tearle is well named, "the Irving of the provinces," although the methods of the two actors and their personalities are by no means similar. Mr. Tearle, moreover, is not a provincial actor because London does not like him—rather is it he who "doesn't like London." For he has had many tempting offers in his time to come to "town," and settle down as a London actor; but they have never induced him to desert his provincial friends, to whose taste for the serious drama the continued success of his excellent repertoire company is an eloquent witness. It is a moot question whether Mr. Tearle is to be more congratulated on his popularity in the provinces, or provincial playgoers on the fact that they are privileged every season to witness some of the finest of Shakespeare's works, handsomely mounted and excellently played by Mr. Tearle and his company. As an actor, Mr. Tearle possesses physical advantages hardly inferior to those which contributed to the success and celebrity of Salvini, while he brings to bear on his work a mind deeply in sympathy with the creations of his author, and surcharged with a passion for the poetical drama. His Virginius is one of the finest performances on the English stage to-day; so is his King Lear, that most trying of Shakespearian parts; his Othello, too, is one of the noblest, one of the most tragic we have seen; his Hamlet is thoughtful and studious; and his Ingomar is as near perfection as a dramatic impersonation might be. As a naturally robust actor, Mr. Tearle's early manner scarcely admitted of these encomiums; but no one who has studied his performance of recent years can fail to appreciate the nice artistic restraint with which he holds his more vigorous powers in reserve.

Born at Plymouth in March 1852, Mr. Tearle is still a comparatively young man; but the larger part of his life has been spent before the footlights, and his present eminent position was only attained after years of incessant industry and close application to his art. He was very fond of reciting as a youth, and in his young days in Liverpool, whither his people had removed from Plymouth, he frequently figured at penny readings, at which, by the way, he had a companion in Hall Caine, who has since become so famous as a novelist. "His first appearance on any stage," as the familiar legend runs, took place on the occasion of "Julius Cæsar" being performed by the students of St. Francis Xavier's College, Liverpool, when young Osmond undertook the part of Trebonius; but it was on the 26th of March 1869, when he had just completed his seventeenth year, that he made his first professional appearance at the old Adelphi, Liverpool, taking the character of Guildenstern in "Hamlet." His début seems to have been very satisfactory to all parties, and the late Barry Sullivan came to take a warm interest in his welfare; indeed it was through the good offices of that excellent old tragedian that Mr. Tearle secured his first engagement to appear in leading parts at Aberdeen, when he was only nineteen years of age. It was at this time, too, in the vacation of 1871, when the young actor was filling a temporary engagement at Warrington, that he made his first appearance as Hamlet. Six years in the provinces, playing in all kinds of pieces, and in all kinds of places—fifteen parts in one week was, Mr. Tearle tells me, his tale of work during an engagement at Greenock in those days, while at the same place he also played female parts in the pantomimes, and appeared in a genuine "play without words"—then he made his way to London. His first appearance here was at the Gaiety—before that house had become a place of mere buffoonery, of course—in a play called "Rose Michel," which was an unqualified failure, only running one week instead of the seven for which the company was engaged; so that Mr. Tearle appeared in several other pieces at the famous theatre in the Strand before the termination of his engagement there. A tour with Mrs. John Wood followed, Mr. Tearle playing Charles Surface and other leading parts; then back to London again, where he appeared with Joseph Jefferson in "Rip Van Winkle," at the Princess's.

During the next eight years the greater part of his time was spent in America, his first five seasons there being at Wallack's Theatre in New York, where he opened as Jaques in "As You Like It" and, among many other parts, played Charles Surface, and Alfred Evelyn ("Money"), being the "original" in America of Sir Horace Welby in "Forget-me-Not," Clement Huntingford in "The World," Frank Darlington in "Youth," and Wilfrid Denver in "The Silver King." The remainder of his transatlantic career was mainly passed under the banner of Mr. Wallack, but one of his most important engagements was for a term of twenty weeks at New Orleans, where he played Myles-na-Coppaleen in "The Colleen Bawn," and Shaun the Post in "Arrah-na-Pogue." It was shortly after his return from America that he set about the organisation of his Shakespearian company, which has become one of the recognised institutions of the provincial stage, and a visit from which is necessary to the completeness of the season in every town of importance in the United Kingdom—excepting the Metropolis, of course. Mr. Tearle's company has on two occasions given the memorial performances at Stratford-on-Avon. In 1888 he played "Henry VI." and "Julius Cæsar" there, and in the succeeding year he staged "King John" and "The Two Gentlemen of Verona." It was said at the time of his performing the first-named work, "Henry VI.," that it had not been placed on the stage from the poet's day till then, while, on the other hand, it was as stoutly maintained that it had been performed last century. I am not aware that the point has been definitely settled the one way or the other; but there is no doubt that the play has seldom, if ever, been seen on the stage since Shakespeare's day, and, with the exception of Mr. Tearle's historical performance, certainly not within the recollection of any living playgoer.

In the course of a very interesting chat with Mr. Tearle, concerning actors and the art of acting, I gleaned much that may be of interest to my readers. My object was not merely to discover when the eminent tragedian was born, and where he was brought up, nor to bring the X rays of investigation to bear upon his corporeal person, and so to find out what he had for breakfast, but to elicit from him his opinions and impressions on matters of use to the stage aspirant, and of interest to the playgoer and the general reader. Beginning at the beginning, which is a good plan to follow in everything one has to do, I first raised the question of the stage aspirant—his number, his character, his fate.

"As regards aspirants," said Mr. Tearle, "there is no lack of them, I need scarcely say. Nor need I emphasise the fact that my almost invariable answer to those who write wanting to go on the stage, is to advise them to stick to whatever business they may be in rather than enter upon a career in which success only comes after long years of toil and hardship, and sometimes not even then. For I know many good actors and actresses, men and women of ripe experience and great natural ability, who find it a hard battle to eke out a livelihood on the stage. And in this connection, let me say that, while it has always been a source of the greatest pleasure to me to guide the footsteps of an ambitious and earnest young histrion, I can look with almost as much satisfaction on cases where a stage-struck youth, who showed no great dramatic instinct, and to whom the years of strife at the bottom of the ladder would have been disastrous, if not absolutely fatal, has been sensible enough to take my advice and to plod on at his trade or profession.

"Those whom I admit into my company from time to time are, as a rule, young men and women who are fully and seriously determined to fight the battle for a position on the stage, and imbued with an intense love of the actor's calling. They are not merely anxious to strut about in pretty and attractive dresses and make-up their faces; and, as a general rule, they have the unmistakable aptitude for the work. A few, a very few, trials serve to convince me on these points; and if the aspirant is found to be wanting in any of those essentials, well, he or she goes back to private life—at least, so far as my company is concerned. And I do not hesitate in this respect, as I am thoroughly convinced that the greatest service a theatrical manager can do to young persons who are not fitted for the stage is to tell them so in the plainest possible words. But I must say how pleasing it is to find that the great majority of those who are anxious to get into repertoire companies, such as my own, are young people whose main desire is to do good, honest work, to gain experience in the plays of Shakespeare and the other standard authors. It would be an easy matter—that is, so far as the supply of willing young actors is concerned—to organise twenty companies out of the many applicants for admission into the one which I control.

"No; my experience is that the beginner on the stage is not only ready and willing to accept advice from those who are competent to give it, but that he is anxious to receive it. I can only think of one of the many who have gone through my hands, who did not receive with sincere thanks all the instruction it was within my power to impart. And in the case I speak of he always did what I told him, although his manner left the lurking suspicion that he was not entirely satisfied my way was better than his own! But the studious young man or woman, for whom you are able to throw a new light on to some passage in Shakespeare, at once feels the value of your assistance, and will never hesitate to come to you again when in doubt as to the inner meaning of a line or passage, which it is the actor's duty to discover and present to his audience.

"After the dramatic instinct, the next great essential is application. There are many good actors who, lacking industry, lacking the power of applying themselves to the constant study of all kinds of parts in addition to those they may be playing, never rise to any eminence. That is to say, a man may be an excellent Iago, a capital Buckingham, a fiery Macduff, a manly Laertes, or a delightful Mercutio, and yet, at a pinch, he might not be able to play Othello, Richard, Macbeth, Hamlet, or Romeo; while one who had never even played any of the second rôles, but, though filling minor characters, had applied himself assiduously to the study of the principal parts, might be able to take them up and make a creditable appearance at very short notice. I myself first played Hamlet under such circumstances, having studied the part long before there seemed any likelihood of my having a chance to play it. And only the other week a young lady in my company surprised us all by coming forward and offering to play such heavy parts as Parthenia ('Ingomar'), Ophelia, Desdemona, Portia, Juliet, and Pauline ('Lady of Lyons'), owing to the illness of the lady who was cast for these. And it said not a little for the assiduity with which this young lady, who had only been in the habit of playing the Actress in the play scene of 'Hamlet,' the Gentlewoman in 'Macbeth,' and such minor parts, must have been studying, that she acquitted herself with the highest credit in the important and difficult rôles I have mentioned, and added Virginia ('Virginius') and Miss Hardcastle ('She Stoops to Conquer') to them the following week. That is the way to win success—constant application, continual study, with a view to playing more important parts than those in which you may be for the time appearing.

"I certainly believe in amateur dramatic societies. They do a great deal of good, and they can do no harm. Many of my people have come to me through them; many of our leading actors were amateurs once. In my young days I was an amateur too. The membership of such societies, and the parts one gets the chance of playing, soon show whether or not one has any aptitude for the stage if one's inclinations should lie that way. But what is still more important is the fact, that the amateur dramatic club cultivates a taste for the drama among its members and their friends, and I do not think it is the means of sending useless and incapable aspirants to the stage-door. For, as I have said, it enables young people to discover, to some extent at least, the ability that is in them; and while the verdict of an audience on an amateur performance is always unreliable for many reasons, it cannot be said that the club encourages those without ability to dream of the regular footlights, while it provides a channel for the pleasurable use of what dramatic talent a young man or woman may have, without imposing the hardships inseparable from a professional career. At the worst, the amateur dramatic club is much better for a young man than the billiard room, or the race-course; it cannot degrade—it must elevate.

"Long runs! Why, they are the curse of modern acting. Playing one part for hundreds of consecutive nights must inevitably result either in slovenliness or mechanicalness. That is too self-evident to require proof. What is wanted is variety of work, and in this regard it is doubtful whether the experience to be obtained in a good repertoire company nowadays is not, in some respects, even better than that of the old stock-companies, where the work was rough and ready, and the time given to study quite insufficient. My repertoire, for instance, includes a large number of Shakespearian and other 'legitimate' plays, which are all staged from time to time, the programme being judiciously varied on each return visit to this town or that. As a general rule we produce six different plays each week we are on tour, the tour lasting for nearly ten months of the year; so that the members of the company have an abundant variety of work and adequate time for study as well. And this was not the case in the old stock days; there was, to be sure, no lack of work then; but the time for study did not exist; or it was even smaller than the small remuneration which rewarded the efforts of the actor. Now, in Aberdeen, where we spent three weeks this tour (Spring 1896), we staged no fewer than thirteen different plays. I am not aware that any other of the repertoire companies at present 'on the road' gives so much variety—at any rate, in the course of three short weeks. I need scarcely point out the immense advantage which accrues to the young actor by such a frequent 'change of bill' within so short a time. As all the plays in my repertoire are known, more or less, to the actors engaged, the hasty and incomplete study of the old stock days is thus obviated.

"Yes, I suppose I am an enthusiast for Shakespeare. But who is not that has once felt the magic of his words? Why, it is one of the greatest pleasures I know to speak the magnificent lines of the master, and to endeavour to realise on the stage the characters which they suggest. After one has been accustomed to play in Shakespeare he takes ill with the prosy prattle of modern dramatists. In fact, I have had letters not a few from former members of my company, who have gone to London theatres where the works of present-day playwrights are performed, and they have sighed to be back again speaking the musical words of the master, instead of having to talk the stuff which is placed in their mouths by the dramatists of to-day. Shakespeare is our greatest treasure; and in my opinion a thorough grounding in his plays is the best foundation for an actor's career. And this, I think, is acknowledged by all actors of experience. At any rate, I may say, without egotism, that a young actor who has been some time in such a company as mine possesses the best of testimonials for admission to a metropolitan company; and it has been a source of great satisfaction to me to watch the after careers in London of many who have served their theatrical apprenticeship under my direction.

"Talking about the teaching of acting, my opinion on that point has always been fixed, and has deepened with years. Acting cannot be taught. Acting is the man. If one has the ability to understand character, and to impersonate it, there are scores of things which can be and must be taught before such an one can become a finished actor; but without the natural ability all teaching is absolute waste of time. A man must *feel* the character he is portraying; he must get inside of it before he can make his audience feel. We can teach a man how to pronounce his words, how to modulate his voice, how to bear himself on the stage, how to dress in keeping with his part; but we cannot teach him how to put the *soul* into his acting if he is not endowed with that gift already. All that can be taught an actor appeals only to the eye of his audience, but he must himself supply that subtle 'sympathy' which completes the illusion and makes the *audience feel* that he is the man he pretends to be. Thus, I entirely disagree with the theory that the greatest actor is he who does not feel his parts. For myself, I consider I have failed in my purpose if I have not got completely into the spirit of my part; and when one is representing a passion, one does not pause to consider how many inches he will lift his arm this way or that, how many steps he will take in going from one point to another. Still you must never lose control of yourself. What is required is to represent nature, and in nature a man in a passion does not do set things, nor move by clock-work; the actor has, therefore, to be true to nature, and if he has entered into the soul of the part, his movements and actions will be in accordance therewith. Once again, acting cannot be taught. Given the indispensable dramatic flame, by careful tending it can be nursed into a fire. Time and experience are the best teachers."

Osmond Tearle